THE LIGHT

THE LIGHT

by
Alice Lauffer Mowery
in association with
Kate Burgess

VANTAGE PRESS
New York   Washington   Atlanta   Hollywood

Verses marked LB are taken from *The Living Bible,* copyright 1971 by Tyndale House Publishers, Wheaton, Illinois, Used by permission.

FIRST EDITION

All rights reserved, including the right of reproduction in whole or in part in any form.

Copyright © 1978 by Alice Lauffer Mowery

Published by Vantage Press, Inc.
516 West 34th Street, New York, New York 10001

Manufactured in the United States of America
Standard Book Number 533-03021-8

Notice among yourselves, Dear Brothers, that few of you who follow Christ have big names or power or wealth. (I Corinthians 1:26 LB)

To all God's little people whom He shall raise up for His Glory.

To Donna—who introduced me to Jesus. God's Grace be with you through Eternity.

Preface

I feel that this book must be written. Our Lord has laid a burden on my heart to share with others His great gifts that *He* will give to others—He wants to give to all, and in some small way, maybe this testimony will help you to meet Jesus personally. Maybe it will help just one person who is searching as I was. *It's so easy* when you know how—we didn't know how.

All you need to know is that, Jesus saves. He is the Lord. He wants to forgive *all*. Yes, I said *all* of your sins. He wants to live in your heart. Just ask Him in; that's all. Just accept Him as your Lord and Saviour, and invite Him to come in. I promise, He will.

The Light is the name that the Holy Spirit seemed to guide me to write as a title for this book. "The Light" is the presence of Jesus. It is not of this world, so it's hard to describe. It's very soft, yet very bright. It's golden, but it seems to be of many different shades of gold, all interlaced together. It seems to enfold you. It's all around you, yet it's all inside you at the same time. It is utter and complete peace and joy, complete freedom from fear, complete rest such as I have never known.

Even now, trying with all my heart, to serve our Lord, and with the peace He has given to me, it is not anything like the peace of the Light. It seems to glow like nothing man can make, and yet, even then, its glow is soft. It is so thick, you can feel it inside and outside of your body, and yet it floats like a cloud, and you float in and with it: like you are a part of it. There is no audible sound, yet you know somehow, everything. It seems as if you just know *all*. And if you let Jesus live in you, you will know all. He was here before the creation of this world and He will be here into eternity.

John 12:46 says, "I have come as a Light into the world that whoever believeth on me shall not wonder in darkness."

THE LIGHT

Chapter One

My life, before I met Jesus, was unimportant. But, maybe a brief glimpse of what I was, will clarify my story.

I was born and raised in Dutch country in Pennsylvania by loving, middle-class parents who gave me every advantage that they could.

My earliest memory of Jesus was on my loving grandmother's lap. Her gentle voice, reading her Bible to me and singing hymns all day as she worked, are a treasure to me. When I tried reading the Bible, beginning always with the Old Testament I seemed to find a wrathful God. I can tell you that I was more than a little afraid of this God and his anger. I met His Son, Jesus, many years later, and there is no fear or wrath when you meet our Saviour. *Then* you know that there is no fear of God's wrath. Jesus is our advocate, our counselor in Heaven. This is written for the Glory of the Lord, and to help any or all who read it to meet and know Jesus. See John 14:6.

I had a rather strict upbringing, but full of love and happiness. My only sister was born when I was 14 and I adored her. I felt like a second mother to her. I met and married a quiet, gentle man of 25 when I was 16: a man who had been raised much like I was. In this, I mean that he was brought up by the Old Testament, and he too, did not know Jesus personally as his Saviour.

I was overweight most of the first thirty-five years of my life, and because of this, I was very insecure. This started a pattern of worrying over every little thing, and feelings of being laughed at, which was to follow me for forty-three years of my life, until Jesus released me from that worry. I had a chip on my shoulder, was loud, aggressive and very outspoken. Because of my pride, I hid to the world, a lonely, insecure person inside.

At age 17, I had a slight nervous breakdown. Nothing dramatic, just the pressure of a young wife; keeping house, bills to pay, no money. We've all had these problems. A year later, my parents moved to Albany, New York, and we decided to make a new start and move there too. At this point in my life, even though I didn't know Jesus, I knew of Him, and He was still there, helping me and guiding me to choose the right paths to follow. I can look at all of this in retrospect now, and see just how close to me our Dear Lord was, but at the time, I was unaware of His presence.

My insecurity prohibited me from making any really close friends. I was always so overly critical of them, seeing all of their faults, that no lasting friendships were ever permitted to develop. I was desperately lonely.

Bud and I had all the ups and downs of every other young couple. He went to work for a brush company, loved his job, was set for life there, or so he thought. We scraped, and I do mean scraped enough money together to buy a little house. We assumed that we were the average American young couple, eking out a life for each other, without any real sense of direction.

Anytime that we had our backs to the wall, it seemed that God somehow, came through for us, so we were sure that He was there somewhere. But, after all, we figured that He had a whole world to take care of, so only when we were backed into a corner, could we really ask Him for help.

After eight years of countless prayers, many disappointments, many medical tests, some of you will know the hurt, our yearning for a child was finally relieved. God gave to us the greatest blessing of our lives—a baby girl. Cindy was the delight of our world, and I made a vow to God to try and raise her as a Christian. We sent her to Sunday School and tried to set an example for her. We were a close little family. Our marriage was always special to us and now with our child it seemed to us—almost perfect. The only gift God's given to me that's more precious than Cindy is my salvation and being able to know and serve our Lord Jesus Christ.

Chapter Two

I was asleep one night in my bed, with Bud at my side, and Cindy asleep in her crib next to our bed. I was not aware of waking, but the first thing that I remember was seeing the sky. I was lying on my own bed, but I looked up and saw the night sky, as clearly as if the room had no ceiling. As I continued to look at the sky, a soft ray of golden light descended from the heavens and gradually came down to touch at the side of my bed. As it came down, it widened out at the bottom, and in the center of the light, my Lord slowly descended to stand by my bed, more nobly and majestically than I had ever imagined. His face could not be seen for the radiant light that emanated from it. His hair was golden in color, and a soft halo shown around His whole body. He was dressed in a dazzling white robe, with a brilliant red cloak trailing behind His shoulders. His voice, when He spoke, was so unspeakably soft, that no word could adequately describe it, and I was overcome with the power of His love. To even think of it, these many years later, brings a warm glow to my heart: so strong was this feeling of love. I felt so happy, yet so humble. This was my Lord! I remember Him asking me if I knew who He was, and I said, "Oh yes, you're Jesus, with the lamb." My grandmother had always kept a picture of Jesus holding a lamb in His arms, and this was the clearest recollection of Him that I had. He asked me many times if I loved Him, and I always answered Him, "Oh yes, Lord, you know that I love You." I remember that we talked for a long time, but the rest of the conversation has been blocked out of my mind forever. I can't remember it. But some day I would know what we talked of. I will never forget the tremendously powerful feeling of His love for me, and mine for Him.

It was unlike anything I had ever felt, no human ecstasy could ever compare to the unrestrained love of our Lord. It is something that doesn't leave you; it clings to your every fiber, and it makes you just want to submit yourself entirely to Him. After we finished talking, He ascended up the ray of light just as He had come down, and I was left with my thoughts. *It was Jesus. He really talked with me. He loves me! He wants me! Should I tell anyone? It's too personal—they will think that I was dreaming. I don't understand all of this, but I am so happy that it happened.*

I recall, that for weeks after the vision, I would go into my room and stand in the same spot as Jesus had stood, and I could still feel His presence there: so powerful is His love.

Did I accept Jesus as my Saviour then? I just don't know. You see, I had no one to teach or guide me. But I feel now, that I did accept Him and would have served Him had I known how. You will see this as you read on. He never left me, from that vision on. See Romans 10:20. I kept this to myself for 17 years, not daring to tell a soul. Now, with our Lord's help, I am telling all.

After the visit from my Lord, I was scheduled to have major surgery, so a little medical history here should help to keep the story straight. I was constantly nervous; I had been treated with tranquilizers for years. There was a disc out of place in my lower spine. This was especially painful and I was treated many times for it. As the years wore on, my body began to build up certain resistances to drugs, and also many allergies were building up. I was allergic to bee stings. If I was stung, I had one hour to get to the hospital or die. Any amount of alcohol would send me to the doctor, and my sight would be affected for days after. All drugs had to be tested before being used on me, as more and more often I went into shock whenever a new drug was used.

During this time, I suffered from a gall bladder condition, for which I refused surgery, being afraid more of the operation than of the discomfort of the bad gall bladder. But at age 28, when my daughter was just three years old, I had no choice. I could no longer survive on the crackers and tea which had been my diet for the past five months. My daughter needed a full-time mother, not one weak from malnutrition. So, with misgivings, I entered the hospital and had surgery.

The evening after the surgery, the nurse gave me a shot of penicillin to ward off any infections. Remember my allergies. Well, they just loved the penicillin. By that night, I was too sick to even know if it had affected me. I shared the room with another woman who also had surgery done on her legs that same day. During the night the second shot was given to me. May the Lord guide me in the telling of this.

I was completely helpless—tubes in my sides—each arm strapped down with intravenous, a dark room, middle of the night, my roommate in a drugged sleep. The nurse gave me the shot by flashlight, and left.

I was on fire from head to toe. I couldn't breathe. It felt as if I were going to burst. I tried to call the nurse, but had no breath to yell, when suddenly, I left that body.

I won't say that it felt as if I had left my body, I did leave my body. I don't know how; I don't know why, but I do know what happened next. Suddenly, a soft, bright, warm light was there in the room, and I became a part of the light, at peace, without fear, calm, at rest. The Light and I as one, floated above the bed. I felt so sorry for Alice. She was in such torment. I kept repeating to my Light, she's so sick, she hurts so bad.

I have no way of telling how long I was suspended like that. Was it an hour? Was it a minute? I don't know, but, suddenly the light woke my roommate. I saw her awaken. She looked over at me in the bed (she could not see the real me), thought I was dead, and not being able to walk, started screaming. At that point, the Light put me gently back into that tormented body. I have no memory of the next few hours. You may say that it was a dream. Well, would a dream, a figment of someone's imagination fill half the room with light, a light so strong that it woke a person from a drugged sleep? Did I change after that? No, not really. I knew somehow, that it had been of God, this light, but I never really allowed myself to think it out. I guess that I felt that it was something that no one would believe and I tried at first to tell a few people. They said that it was only a dream, but only my loving Bud would believe me. So even though I will never forget it, I kept it to myself just as I had with the vision.

Six days after the surgery, my throat swelled shut so tightly that even my own saliva wouldn't go down. The doctor said that it was nerves and ordered more tranquilizers. As the throat condition became worse, the nurses lost patience with me. I couldn't swallow the pills that were supposed to relieve my "tension" and this only increased the animosity toward me. They thought that I was just acting like a baby. I received very little care. Did God desert me in all of this? Never! In my agony, I was crying, praying; and just then a very important doctor was making some sort of inspection of the hospital facilities, and he "happened" to walk into my room. I do believe that God was using this man that day. The doctor walked over to my bed and asked the nurse what was wrong with me. The nurse explained that it was nerves and that I would not cooperate by taking my pills.

Praise God for this doctor. He reached out and touched my throat with two fingers, turned to the nurse and said, "Call her surgeon at once; take her to X ray. In my opinion she has esophagustus." This is a swelling of the esophagus, very painful, and not uncommon. God worked in many hearts that day. My own doctor apologized and explained that I was not suffering from a bad case of nerves. The nurses who had been so rough and uncaring became tender angels of mercy once again. As you will read on, you will see that God has never left me at any time. I just didn't know that He was there. Praise the Lord!

I thought of this Light many times when I left the hospital. Oh, how I wanted to tell someone and to ask many questions. I did tell Bud and we talked of it and knew God had touched me and given me back my worldly life. We thanked Him and returned to our normal family life. Our life was changed by this first surgery. Our love for each other had been tested and came through stronger than ever. We had been blessed in many ways.

Chapter Three

After leaving the hospital, my condition failed to improve. I was anemic, and my allergies steadily grew worse. My nerves were bad, very bad, and consequently, I was depressed a great deal of the time. Did I blame God? Oh no. In fact, I thanked Him, thinking that by being so very brave through all this pain and suffering I was being a good Christian. How little my life glorified God in those days. I tried to show my husband how very brave I was. I didn't even let him see how much torment I was going through.

Dear, dear Bud never lost patience with me, during all these illnesses. He never lost his temper; God gave him great strength. Sometimes we don't know where extra strength comes from, and we tend to discount it, but believe me, all that patience that Bud showed in those years came from God. He worked hard to pay the medical bills, never complaining of our spartan social life, never mentioning all the sacrifices that he made for me. Yes, God gave Bud great strength, and God gave Bud to me.

I went to church quite often; in fact, I went to several different churches. I seemed to be searching, yet I couldn't figure out what I was searching for, nor could I seem to find it. I feel that the teachings of my youth were blinding to me the real truth about Jesus. I knew that I had lived as close to those teachings as I could have, yet I seemed to know that I was being led. I explained it to myself as having a deep sense of right and wrong, and dismissed it as such.

In all those years, there were many minor surgeries. I don't mention this for pity, but only so that all who read this will know how great and merciful our Lord Jesus is.

Not once, in all those years, could I honestly answer anyone's questions of, "How do you feel Alice?" by saying, "Fine, just fine." No, I never felt complete relief from all my physical ailments. All my operations are on record at the hospital. Many are stamped incurable—I need not go into this now. I want only to show the power and glory of our Lord. All who face surgery, death, worry, pain, troubles, need have no fear. *He* is there. *He* will never leave you. If only I had known this 17 years ago, I could have given many more years of service to my Lord. Trust in the Lord. Obey the Lord. And in all things, praise the Lord!

When our daughter was eight years old, I again entered the hospital for minor surgery. On the morning that I was scheduled to go into surgery, my duodenal ulcer ruptured. Because of my allergies, six specialists and surgeons were called in to figure out how to get me out of this mess. How could they put me under safely? I was allergic to everything. Would my body accept the tube necessary to remove the ulcer? If my body rejected the tube, I would certainly die. I was steadily bleeding to death. After one week, and many consultations, it was decided: the ulcer could not be removed. A new and untried operation (book surgery) would be done. This operation would cut the main nerve in the stomach, the vagus nerve, bend the duodenal tube out of shape to make a pocket to protect the ulcer until it could heal. Loss of blood and extraordinary circumstances made the surgery touch and go.

The ten days before surgery were rough. To say

that I was afraid would be an understatement. But I still felt that I had to act brave. "Don't let it show."

No one knew the agony of body and spirit that I was going through. Did I say no one? That is not entirely correct. God knew. God always knows. And He always does something about it, too. The day before the operation, a kind and loving priest came in to see me. Now, I'm a Protestant, but I have always felt close to a man of the cloth, especially a Catholic priest, and this man was sent from the Lord. He talked to me and I unburdened myself to him. I cried; we prayed. He did not try to convert me; in fact, in his quiet and gentle manner, he went on to tell me of how he grew up, and when and how he found Christ. While he was there, the doctor stepped in and thinking the priest was of my faith, told him just how dangerous the surgery was. Before he left, that dear priest said that he would like to say the special prayer of his faith (the last rites) that would go with me into surgery. You know, that prayer has been completely wiped out of my mind; I do not remember a word of it. I only remember that I had thought that it was the most beautiful prayer that I had ever heard. Before he left, he promised to look in on me in the morning. He was to offer communion to his people, and as I was not of his faith, he could not offer it to me, but he would bless me and make the sign of the cross with his chalice over my head. He explained that to him, the cup was a symbol of holiness, and I felt honored that he would share this with me. He left, and such a wonderful peace descended over me, I fell asleep and slept like a child. True to his word, the good priest was there at 5 A.M., the next morning. One glance at my face told him that God had touched me. I was at peace with the Lord. May God bless that dear priest, wherever he is serving.

During the surgery, one lung collapsed. The second day, brought pneumonia. I was on my way out. My husband almost lived at the hospital. Between working and caring for Cindy, he spent hours praying by my bed. Sometimes I knew that he was there, other times, I did not.

All of you who fear death, please believe what I am about to say. I was unconscious most of the time, so they tell me. I was in such pain that it cannot be described. But then, suddenly, my pain was gone. But I was in total darkness: blackness, such as no night will ever see. The fear in me and around me was impregnable; it was worse than all the nightmares that I've ever had, all rolled into one.

Suddenly, a lovely, soft light wrapped itself around me and in me. It was love, joy, and peace. It was a soft sweet touch of heaven and I knew what it was and where it was leading me, and the joy was so divine, that I cannot describe it. Somehow, beyond the darkness, I heard my husband crying out and holding my hand, begging me not to die, not to leave him, to please come back. Without words being spoken, the Light told me to go back. I did not want to leave this joyful place. I did not want to descend even for a short time, back into the blackness. I did not want to go back to that pain-ridden body, even though I loved my husband very much. Even for Bud, I did not want to return. But the glorious Light of many colors knew best. I went back. It did not force me to return, but seemed to lovingly guide me and advise me to go back.

But be not afraid. Psalm 23:4 says that His promise is—as we walk *through* the valley, He is with us. That great and wondrous Light will come. It will lead the way. It will not leave you in darkness. I didn't know it then, but I know now, that the Light was Jesus.

When Bud left the hospital, that night, he knew that I was dying. He just walked and prayed and begged God not to take me from him and Cindy. A soft light came to him and filled his heart with peace, and he knew that God had said yes to his prayer. It was 12 years later, when both my husband and I knew Jesus personally, that we confessed to each other what each of us had seen and felt that night.

After 4½ weeks in the hospital, I was allowed to go home. I needed constant care and since the hospital was shorthanded, they let me walk out. As Bud and I got to the car I collapsed and hit my head causing a permanent bruise on the back of my skull. The doctors just added this bruise to my file of: "Learn to live with it; cannot be cured." With the back of my head so sore, I couldn't even put a roller in that spot without a headache.

God was all around us, and we didn't even know enough to invite Him into our hearts.

Chapter Four

The year that followed was straight out of a nightmare. My nerves were virtually gone. I was always afraid: of what, I don't know, perhaps, just fear of life itself.

The type of surgery I had required a diet of baby food. I refused to eat, so all food had to be ground up and made soft like liquid. But, the horrible part was that I had no control over my bowels. Just like a baby, I could not leave the house; even a small movement of the car caused a bowel movement. In 6 months I lost 60 pounds. Being overweight, I could afford it. I was sent to a psychiatrist, who, after three visits, assured me that, being in my position, he would be having a nervous breakdown himself, and that it was a medical problem and he could not help me.

My allergies seemed to abound. I was allergic to all pain medicine. I lived on aspirin. I couldn't eat any pork, eggs, milk, lemon sauce or pie. I could not use any sort of hand cream, or lotions; no make-up. I was not bedfast, but needed so much care, that when my parents and sister moved to a very small community outside of Albany, we too, decided to sell, and move closer to them.

Many times I needed their help. The diarrhea never stopped; all food went straight through me, and two years later, I was admitted into the hospital. The first day that I was there I had thirty-six bowel movements. I had lost 90 pounds. Tests started again—what was wrong? Could the stomach nerves be put back together? No they could not, and the ulcer, which had never healed, was still bleeding. After tests, and X rays, it was determined that there was a deformity of the panacrea gland, possibly a tumor or cancer. I was prone to tumors, having had several small ones removed.

Oh, I was frightened! This time I shared the room with a nun's mother, and during the day the sister was there caring for her mother. See, God was at work again, sending someone to care for me spiritually, as well as physically. I was scheduled for some very painful tests to determine what was necessary and between tests, the sister and I talked for many hours. Again God was with me. Sister had been to Lourdes. She had a very small bottle of the holy water from there, and she asked me if I would like her to ask God's blessing on me. She would make the sign of the cross on my forehead with this precious holy water, and I should ask God myself to take care of me. I just repeated over and over again, "Not cancer, anything else, I will bear: not cancer." May God bless that dear sister. Once again I was at peace. Oh, If I had only known how to keep that peace.

The next day I was told, no cancer: an incurable stomach disease and a deformed panacrea gland that secreted too much insulin, which meant that I had to carry rock sugar with me at all times or go into sugar shock, but no cancer. I would just have to learn to live with both. Medical file stamped: *incurable*. The diarrhea could only be slowed down with opium drops; it never stopped.

All these many incurable sicknesses and diseases that I have been talking about are on record as such. I would like to skip this part, about all my illnesses, for actually my life didn't really start until many years later, when I met Jesus on a personal basis and really knew

Him, but to leave these things out would not be the truth, and this is what this book is all about: *truth*.

In the next year the diarrhea slowed to a 6-to-10-times-a-day type of thing. It was to say the least, embarrassing, but not fatal. I continued to lose weight by an average of 4 or 5 pounds a month. All foods gave me an upset stomach, but I was not in terrible pain.

Then a new problem arose. After many months of hemorrhaging, cramps, and so forth, I consulted my family doctor for a boil on the inside gland of my upper left leg. He hospitalized me and called in a specialist. It seemed that I was full of tumors and needed a hysterectomy. For four days I lay with legs elevated refusing to sign the surgery consent forms. Why? Fear. Fear that I would not live, fear that I would live and not be a woman again, some of you know that fear. Oh, if only I had known the Lord Jesus at that time. I would have realized that all my fears were unnecessary. You see, to live with Jesus in your heart is to live without fear. He conquered fear when He died on the cross, and with Him living in us, we too need no longer be trapped by fear. Fear is the devil's way to blind us from the true freedom that Jesus Christ gives.

Again, God sent someone. One of His. Our minister came to see me. He didn't pray, he didn't beg, he just reminded me that I had a dear little girl waiting for me at home and that God had entrusted her to us to raise. I signed the consent forms when he left.

I will not go into all the details, but I was allergic to all the drugs that they tried. I was bleeding to death. The night before the operation, our family doctor visited me and asked that my husband be there. He laid it on the line for us. I had a 50/50 chance. I should put my affairs in order. But I was not afraid. Again, God had given me inner peace. I seemed to be right with this world, and the next also. The doctor explained that this type of surgery, with nothing for pain, could kill me or leave me permanently insane. My mind would block out the intense pain, but as far as coming out of it, well, that was "up to God."

I woke from surgery just as I was being pushed into the intensive care unit. That shook me. After all, I thought that you went in there to die. I was awake only long enough to know that I was being put there, then I remembered nothing. The next thing that I do recall is opening my eyes and seeing the nurse at the desk at the bottom of my bed. She was giving a doctor someone's vital signs over the phone. Being a practical nurse, I knew enough that whoever belonged to those vital signs was on the way out. Then I realized that she was talking about me. I was dying! I tried and tried to scream at her, but no sound came out. "No, no, no," I screamed in my head. "I'm not dying!" How did I know this? My precious Light had not come for me, that's how.

Only God knows why I did not die, but that was all that was important. God did know, and God let me know. My work had not even begun. Recovery from surgery was slow. I was quick-tempered, got hot flashes, and my nerves were, if possible, worse.

Over this period of years that I'm speaking of, whenever I could, I got part-time jobs to help my husband out. Our medical bills were sky high. When times got really tight, it seemed that my health improved just long enough to go to work for a few months. Then, being anemic, having low blood pressure, and all that, the extra work would always wear me down.

It was a vicious cycle, yes, but still, it seemed that I had something or someone with me. Someone not of this world. I was brave, but only because somehow I seemed to know that this was not always going to be like this. I felt that there was something at my very fingertips that I could have for the asking. God forgive me, I did not know what it was.

I had tried over the years, to read my Bible. I understood about 10% of it, so I really didn't try very hard. I prayed, yes. But I prayed to a God of wrath. Even though I prayed to Him, I feared His wrath more than anything. I tried to always live right. Why? Because I was afraid of God's wrath; yet, I can't tell of all the ways, both big and small, that God spoke to me. I knew He cared. Had He not spared me three times? Had He not sent a light to help me? Oh yes. God was always in the back of my mind. Praise God, He is in my heart now.

Chapter Five

Shortly after the surgery, I went shopping with my mother and father. It was one of those days that your memory treasures. The sun filled the beautiful fall day and everyone was relaxed and glad to be together. We joked as we drove into Albany and walked about the stores. Our last stop was at the supermarket, and as I was standing in line behind my parents, I heard a voice speak to me, and I looked around to see who belonged to it. No one was near me, and still the voice went on, "Alice, you are not going to have that 'old man' for very long." It was a loving voice, speaking of my father as the "old man"; I had always called him that. I wondered what that voice could mean. Dad had just had a complete exam in July and was told that his health was perfect. Did I believe my voice? Oh yes. God had been too perfect and always told the truth to me, so I had no reason not to believe His voice. I knew that again God had spoken and that I would lose my dad. I told only Bud.

Three months later the worst was confirmed. Dad had lung cancer. He didn't have too much time to live, but oh, the courage that man had! I could write a million words on his courage, but I'm praying for guidance and only telling my story to show the glory of God in my life. I will only say, that losing dad was a terrible, empty hurt but God was there and He never gives you more than you can bear. When there is a terrible sorrow, God gives you strength like you've never had before. Some people may feel that the strength is acquired, that it comes from within, that it is their own reserve of strength. This is just not so. If God built us humans with an inner reserve, certainly science would have tapped this natural resource and we would be able to use it at will. This strength does not come from us. We do not build up the strength, nor do we store it up for future use. God gives us the strength that we need day by day, hour by hour.

God never fails His children. That's why so many people who live for Jesus never seem to worry. We give it to the Lord. There are many things in life that some of us feel that we cannot handle. We wonder what would happen to us, if by chance the one thing that we dread most would happen. In this case, the Christian has an advantage over any other person. We know from the promises of the Bible that God is in control at all times. You may think the strength that you need is out of reach, but it's there. It's such a comfort. Knowing that this will happen gives one a quiet sense of inner peace that never leaves you. You know that God is going to take care of you. He says He will, and you take Him at His word. Before you know it, He has done just that.

Three months after dad's death, I went to work for an insurance company close to my home. We certainly did need the extra money. I did not ever at any time really feel great, just good enough to get by. I liked my work. Even though some days I could barely put one foot in front of the other, I missed very little work. Here again was something taught to me as a child. My grandparents lived by and taught their children and grandchildren, that "you give an honest day's work for an honest day's pay." Being honest about everything is something that was important to them and to me.

Three months after starting to work again, I needed another operation. The problem, this time, was bladder suspension. Normally this type of surgery is not really dangerous, but remember my allergies. Sodium pentathol was out. I had gone into shock the last time that it was used on me. But still, on the outside I was brave. My family was worried sick. I joked about it, saying that the doctors would use hammers and saws on me. Oh yes, the frightened, insecure Alice was there inside of me screaming. I was determined not to let my fears show. I remember thinking, "Make everyone think that you're brave and strong. Just hold on. Wait till they leave—you know where your help is. Hurry, leave, so I can look out of that window to the sky and start talking to *Him*."

You notice that I still didn't realize that *He* was down here with me. He was way up there somewhere sitting on a throne—watching and listening. At times when I really needed Him, I knew that He heard me. And again, I needed Him. I put all my heart into that prayer as I begged Him to take this fear from me and to give me the courage to face whatever lay ahead. He filled me with peace and told me all was well, everything would go well. And you know, everything *did* go well. God never lies.

After the surgery, I started to have more complications. My stomach was becoming more and more bloated every day. One month after surgery, as the doctor examined me, he looked into my mouth, studied my gums, and called an oral surgeon right away. The oral surgeon X rayed me and told me that I had a fungus eating out my jawbone. How much, they would not know, until they had gone into my mouth to see. Already they knew that it was going to be extensive.

Because of my allergies, regular dentures were out. I was even allergic to the substance put into the mouth for an impression. What could they make my teeth out of? How could all this be done? There were countless problems.

I have to confess something here. My grandmother had cancer of the face, and for all the years of my childhood I remember seeing her with her face eaten away, and sometimes, with just a damp cloth over it. It impressed on my mind such a fear of ever having anything done to my face, that I carried this fear with me into adulthood. I couldn't stand for any one to touch me from the neck up. So, with all things combined, I hit the panic button. Did I have cancer of the jawbone? Would I live through the operation? If I had cancer, did I want to live? I had been told what to expect. I would not look the same when I came out of surgery, as when I went in. Would Bud love me still? With all these scars and diseases? I hit bottom alright. *Be brave*, I told myself. *I can't be brave!* I screamed back. *Oh God, help me, help me!*

If only I had known that Jesus is living within each of His children, my fears would have been calmed instantly. Here I must say that God has a plan for everything. Because my awareness of Jesus came later on in my life, I can look at these events in retrospect and appreciate God's mercy even more.

In desperation, I took the car and went to my dad's grave. There I fell on my knees; daddy's little girl didn't know what to do. I cried, "Daddy, I need you. I don't know what to do. Daddy, if there's a hereafter and you're there, plead for me. Oh God help me. I'm so afraid. Oh, Daddy, help me. Oh, Daddy, if I'm going to die, meet me and lead me there."

I don't know how long I stayed there, crying, begging, pleading, promising to live a better life. I just needed help as I never had before. I came apart at the seams. After awhile, I started to feel more calm. I knew, too, that daddy couldn't help me. But all the fears had gone. If I didn't make it through surgery, I'd be OK. Only the hurt that my family would feel bothered me. If I made it through, I would be OK too. The fluffy white clouds seemed just over my head. The quietness of the cemetery filled my soul. I could sense the love in that cemetery. Only now do I realize who and what it was. It was our Lord.

I felt as if daddy had heard me. Maybe he did, but our Father in Heaven heard me, and that is what is most important. In his great love for us, and in His pity for me, a sinner, He sent me peace. He took away my fears.

Never have I earned these gifts. That's why they are called gifts. They are given to us by God, to use for His glory, and in His way. The gifts of God are free and cannot be earned. God loves us so much that He wants to give us *all*.

I calmly entered the hospital. I didn't like it one bit, but now I accepted it all. Accepting all is the first step in faith. God has plans for all of us, and we must be attuned to His spiritual voice to hear what He has in store for us.

Bud walked beside the stretcher and down the elevator to the door of surgery. He was quite upset, and I recall my last words to him, which were from the Lord, "I will be back." I came back from surgery, and someday soon our Lord Jesus is going to come back to us.

The doctor could give me only enough gas to barely put me out. I was floating just enough to feel all the pain, to know some of what was going on. Later the surgeon told me that he thought he had lost me three separate times. Maybe he thought so, but I knew better.

When the Lord tells you that it's OK, believe!

The plastic teeth were put in, but they didn't fit. 1½ inches of jawbone had been removed, and steel pins driven to hold it all together. No other teeth could be made to fit any better, so they were another torment I had to learn to live with.

After three months, I returned to work. If I thought that I had worked in agony before, it was worse now.

Regardless of my poor health, things seemed to get better for us. We caught up on our bills, which was a relief. We even started to save some money. I got a better job with the company, more pay and less work. But my legs were acting up and spasms would turn my feet upward, so that I could look at the bottom of them, I couldn't go upstairs without having leg cramps. I went back to the doctors for more tests. It was a disease of the nerves. One of the leg nerves was 50% dead and the other leg was starting to show signs of nerve damage too. No cure. Allergic to pain pills. Only muscle relaxers could offer some relief. My medical file again read: *incurable*.

Even when I didn't have spasms, my legs ached all the time, day or night. I didn't sleep well and could not take sleeping pills to help. I also had a bad back. Any position which relieved my legs would hurt my back. Again a vicious cycle.

The big old house that we were living in had three floors. We decided to sell and find something smaller and on one floor. Doctors told me that in a few year's time I would be in a wheelchair. To save unnecessary pain, the elimination of the stairs was imperative.

We put the house up for sale and ordered a little modular to be built right next door. We then went on vacation. When we returned in less than a week the house was sold and our modular wasn't ready. To add to all the evils, there was a letter in the mail waiting for Bud. The company that he had been with for 23 years was moving to Kansas. He was out of a job.

Bud's health had always been excellent, but that year it was below par. He had kidney stones removed, the gout, and now, no job. Well, it didn't matter how I felt, I had to work. How foolish we were! We put every penny that we could in the bank. We cut corners. We worried. We forgot God. We forgot to take our problems to Him. We just worried our way through it all. Just put yourself in our shoes for a minute, and think of how it must have been. Bud's pride was crushed because of the loss of his job. He had always been able to provide for us.

Bud finally got a job as a bank guard. He worked all sorts of odd hours. His days off were in the middle of the week, and mine were on the weekend. We rarely were with each other and our family life just fell apart. After a year he got a job as a custodian. His hours were still not regular, but he did have weekends off. At least we could have those times together as a family.

Chapter Six

Now, dear God, please bless the writing of what is to follow. May Your Holy Spirit, tell it like it is, to Your Glory. Amen.

About this time, I started having pain in my right arm, shoulder and chest. When I used my right hand, the pain got worse. My job was payroll, so all day I used my right hand and arm. I didn't say anything, just suffered in silence, being the martyr, until one day the pain was so serious that I couldn't breathe. I drove myself into the emergency room and again, the series of endless tests, specialists, X rays, and visits to the heart specialist began. I have an extra rib and it presses on the muscle of the heart. Was that it? No, the doctors said. My life was again turned upside down. After five weeks, they found the cause of the problem: tendonitis—a calcium deposit locking the shoulder and shortening the tendon leading up the neck and the entire length of my right arm.

I was ordered into physical therapy and anyone who has been through therapy knows how much suffering goes on in there. You scream with the pain. You pray that you could just faint and get out of it. You don't want to go to sleep at night, knowing that in the morning you will have to face therapy again. I went through 10 days of therapy, and 10 days of complete rest for six months.

I came as near to giving up as I ever had or ever will. I could not, nor would not, learn to live with one more thing. I wanted out. I'd had it! There was pain everywhere—my head, face, stomach, back, legs and now the arm, shoulder and chest.

Did I think of taking my life? Yes, many, many times, and the only reason that I didn't was pure selfishness. I was afraid of what God would have to say about that.

It was not a sin that you could ask forgiveness for. Would I go straight to hell? This being a possibility, I decided to hang in there for a little longer.

In these six months, there had been a big change in my kid sister. She got religion. I was glad. After all, when she was in high school, for awhile, she didn't really believe in God, so if she believed now, well, that was great! The only disquieting part about it was that she kept sweetly trying to tell me, who for 16 years, was always being blessed. She had a lot of nerve.

She was saying all sorts of crazy things that I just couldn't swallow: things like, "Your sins will all be forgiven, even the sins that you haven't committed yet."

Now, I won't listen to talk like that, why, it's way-out. After all, everybody knows, that if you're going to sin, that you are going to have to pay for it. You *have* to pay for it, don't you? And what's this bull about turning everything over to the Lord? Now, everyone knows that He hasn't time to listen to every little whimper. Right? After all, I kept telling myself, doesn't it say that God helps them who help themselves? What do you mean—I'm not a Christian? I live better than most of those people in church.

What's all this about the Spirit of the Lord entering into me? What is this crazy kid talking about? What does she mean, "We must let the Spirit of the Lord come into our church"?

Oh brother, I thought, *now, that's going too far. Now*

I'm going to have to give it to her good!

I said, *You want to believe all of this stuff? Well, fine, but don't you ever shove it down people's throats. That's their church. If you don't like it the way it is, leave.*

I really came down hard on her. How could I know that she was talking about one of the no, let me say, the greatest truths of all time. Jesus is Lord. Jesus lives in every Christian's heart. He does His work through them. All you have to do is to ask Him to come into your heart. That's as simple as it was, but without believing it, you are missing the point.

Well, my sister kept up her chatter, visiting and helping me three or four times a week, always quiet and sweet, never overbearing, just irritating to me, the good Christian woman that I thought that I was. Would I go to Bible study with her? Well, "Alright," I said, "I know most of the people, I don't care for them, but I know them, and if no one bumps my right side, I'll sit through the thing." But I went only because she was having it at my mother's house and besides, it was a going away party for a special young man, who to me at that time, was someone so special, so holy, that he surely must walk next to God Himself. I am taking the time to say here, that Hank *is* all of those things, but he's not next to God. He is just one person, overflowing with the Spirit of God, something which we all, each and everyone of us, can be if only we ask.

But I went. I didn't join in, after all, I knew those people. Some of them, to tell the truth, I didn't even like. No, the absolute truth is, I couldn't stand a couple of them. Well, they sang songs like "Lets Just Praise the Lord" and they shut their eyes and raised their arms. I remember thinking, *Who are they kidding, these Holy people? Hey, I know that one, and he's not kidding me. What a silly show. There's no way that I want any part of this crew!*

They'll have to stop soon, and eat those special cakes that were out in the kitchen. Then my sister can take me home, and I can tell her what I think of this silly stupid acting bunch of people.

Well, they started moving out into the kitchen, so to protect my shoulder, I moved out into the living room, to a big chair in the corner, so that no one could bump my arm. Then, a gal I had known for 10 years and worked with at the insurance company, asked how I was. I told her that the day before the therapist had ordered more therapy and I had refused, my nerves being shot. Ten more days of that therapy and I knew that I'd either have killed myself or gone crazy. The doctor had gone into the waiting room to talk to Bud, explaining that even though I was in great pain, and he could give me nothing more that aspirin, it was imperative for me to continue the therapy, or I'd never use my arm again. (Praise God, that arm is writing this down.) Bud should bring me back in a week. I had just one week to get myself calmed down and go into therapy again for another two weeks.

But this gal at the Bible study said, "We'll pray and lay hands on you."

I said, "I'm almost desperate enough to try it." But I was just being polite; after all, if I had said what I really thought, I would have insulted her. But, before I could stop her, she announced that we were going to pray for Alice.

How did I get myself into this mess? I thought. *How do I get out of it?*

Praise God that Gladys is not the type to take no for an answer. I found myself sitting on a chair in the middle of the room and these silly people were going to put their hands on me. Well, you don't touch me anywhere that you feel like it, and you surely don't dare touch my shoulder, which I told them, not too nicely.

Well, those hands came down on me—my legs, my

left arm, my feet, my head, and then they started to pray.

Well, I guess I should put my head down, I thought. *After all, you can sit here and let them do their thing, can't you? No, I can't. This is silly. I just want to go back and sit down, and be left alone. Listen to them mutter!*

Mom's little dog is sick, she'd better take her to the vet. Oh, why don't they shut up? If only I hadn't come, this is all so embarrassing. What do they expect me to do? Should I say thank you? When will this be over? When do they say Amen?

Suddenly two hands were touching my shoulder and neck. I thought, *I told them not to do that. Why doesn't it hurt? They have their hands right there, and it should hurt!*

The next thing I knew, a red hot feeling started at my hand and went straight up the arm into the shoulder, through the shoulder, and up my neck and out the top of my head. At this time, everyone was saying, "Thank you, Jesus. Amen."

I was free—I could get up from that chair. They were done. Boy! I was glad that no one asked me how I felt. For that matter, no one said anything. They simply went back to eating their cake and I went back to my chair in the corner.

What kind of people are they? I kept saying to myself. *Am I supposed to feel better? What was that hot feeling I'd had? Aren't they curious? Why, they're leaving, and all that they're saying to me is* Good-bye. *Talk about a bunch of kooks, these people have the corner on the market.* Praise the Lord, that I'm one of those kooks now.

By that time, my husband was off work, so he came and picked me up. On the way home, I mentioned that the bunch had prayed for my healing.

"But, don't ask me any questions," I said. Bud kept silent.

That night, I noticed that the covers didn't seem to

hurt my shoulder like they had for six months. I could pull them all the way up to my neck, the way that I liked, and it didn't hurt me at all. I slept all night through, which was in itself, a miracle.

The next morning, I went into the kitchen as usual, walked in to the cupboard and reached up for a cup. I stopped. I looked at my arm. My right arm moved all by itself! I turned to Bud, and the smile on his face told me that he too, had noticed. I caught a glimpse of his lips forming the words, "Thank you God!"

I said to him, "I don't want to talk about it." You see, I couldn't. How had it happened? Why? Who? Was it real? Would the pain come back? What did that group have? Does the Lord heal you even if you don't believe in the people praying for you? Does He? Had He? Was it all in my mind? What would the doctor say? Should I try to use it? I remember saying, "Dear God, what has happened to me? Why me God? I'm not a good person like my grandmother was. I haven't even been to church for a year."

I was totally confused. The only thing that I was sure of, was that each day, my arm got a little better, and after three days, it really didn't hurt too much. I could comb my hair. I could finally wash my face with both hands. What was going on?

On Wednesday, I kept the doctor's appointment. His face was full of pity for me as he greeted me at the door and asked how I was. In answer, I raised my arm and placed my finger on the top of my head. I'll never forget his face at that moment. He and his assistant went over me with a fine-tooth comb. It seemed that one inch of calcium had split the entire length of the shoulder, and it can be seen to this day, a lovely groove, right there in the center of my shoulder. Did I explain it to him? How could I? He said that the pain must have been unbearable when it broke. If only he knew, if only I had told him, when the Lord heals, there is no pain.

Chapter Seven

For three weeks, I thought and thought. On Sunday, I went to church. One of the men who had dared to put his hand on my neck, came up to me to say hello. I said, quietly, "Art, did you know that I was healed?"

He just said, "Yes." Nothing else.

Well now, I thought, *that's all? How did he know? Probably my sister told him.*

That afternoon, I asked my sister, "Did you tell Art that I was healed?"

She said, "No," and then we dropped it.

How did he know? Who told him?

My sister continued to visit two or three nights a week. She talked more of her way-out Jesus stuff. Remember how I worried over my illnesses, bills and other problems? Well, she said things like, "Give your worry to the Lord. Let go of it."

"What does she mean, 'give it to the Lord'? After all, you don't just wrap it up and mail it off to Him. What *was* she talking about?"

She kept saying, "Ask Jesus in. Ask Him in."

"Where? How? Why?"

"Are you sorry that you have sinned?" she asked.

"Of course," I said.

"Then say, 'Lord forgive me' and invite Him in."

Well, this kid did have something that I did not have. A new deep inner strength, a soft glow when she said the word Jesus. She had a strong conviction of what to do with her life. Did I want it? Later on, we talked of my healing. She explained that the people didn't heal me; it didn't matter if I believed in them, or even liked them; they were only serving the Lord. *He* heals. Boy, that was a relief. Now, I know how I was healed. But why? Oh, I thought of many reasons—a reward for seventeen years—wrong, Alice. He wanted me, and this was His way of getting me. Wrong again, Alice. He loves, and wants us all. Right.

OK, I said to myself. *I won't tell anyone, but I'll invite Him.*

I did just that. I asked the Lord Jesus to come into my heart every day for a week. Nothing happened. I got a little desperate. I didn't say, "I invite you in," I said, "Jesus, I'm begging you—come in. Come in. Please come in." Nothing happened.

Did I say nothing? Well, I went back to that Bible study group and something was different. I not only didn't feel dislike for everyone there, but slowly I started to love them. Real love, such as I had never felt. It is a different love than for family. If they were sick or troubled I hurt for them; I wanted to just hug them, and tell them how much I loved them. After three or four weeks I even found myself praying for them. Why they were not kooks, but lovely people, full of love and joy in their Lord. Notice I said *their* Lord. I still didn't know that our dear Jesus had come into my heart just as soon as I had asked Him.

All at once I realized that my constant worrying was gone. When had it gone? Who cared? Hallelujah! It's gone. Why, if I trust You, Jesus, I don't have to worry, and all my worry wouldn't change anything anyway, would it? So that was what my sister meant! "Give it to the Lord." Would I ever! All of it. When I started to worry, I'd stop and say, "Jesus, it's in Your hands. Thank You." The worry and the fear would go away. See Luke 12:25–26.

All of my life, I had been afraid—when my husband

or daughter left the house—fear that they would be hurt or worse would haunt me. I took trips only when I had to. The reason: fear of an accident. If the wind started to blow, I was afraid. If Bud got sick, I was afraid. I was afraid that we would not have enough money to live on. Fear, fear fear. Always fear. And now, the fear was gone! Praise God. He took the fear and put peace and trust in its place.

Wow! I've got something here; I want more of it. Why, I even understand some of the Bible now. It seemed to be talking right to me. Why, I even felt a soft lovely inner peace that told me that Jesus' Spirit was there.

I wondered how you got more of this Spirit. I never was one to go halfway. I still didn't understand everything that I read. OK, kid sister, let's talk some more. How do you understand the Bible?

"Simple," she said. "Before you open it, just ask the Lord to open it up to you as you read."

Can she really know what she's talking about? I thought. *Why, that's so simple.*

Try it, You'll like it. It works!

"Well now, this Spirit inside me is really growing. I feel It. It's there, and it seems to help me through even little tiny problems. I feel an inner joy, a quiet place of rest that never leaves me, a fresh new love of everything." Someone said to me, "You have the patience of a saint," and suddenly, I realized that I had. Me, who had always been so impatient in everything.

It must be Jesus, I thought. *He did come in when I asked Him. He had given all this to me so slowly* over a period of several months, so gently, that I had not been aware of changing.

Chapter Eight

We went to Pennsylvania for our vacation. We have a small trailer parked next to Bud's mother's. When I got out of the car, I felt such love for my mother-in-law, I was overwhelmed. *Why*, I thought, *had we not gotten along for 26 years? Why, she was the greatest!* I just loved her with all my heart. I thank Jesus for giving me this deep love for Mom. We have shared beautiful hours together talking of our Lord. My blindness over 26 years almost made me lose the chance to love her. Praise God!

As I lay asleep there one night, pain woke me. "Oh, God," I said, "that ulcer has burst again." I knew that pain, no one had to tell me what it was. I couldn't move. I couldn't breathe. I couldn't even call Bud. "Oh Jesus," I cried, "what can I do? Help me."

Then a strong thought came over me, and I obeyed it. Putting my hand over my waist, I said, "In the name of Jesus Christ, I command you to leave." John 14:14 says, "Yes, ask anything, using My name, and I will do it!" (Reach Out.)

The pain was gone. My stomach wasn't even sore. I wondered, *Should I tell anyone? Would they believe me? Would they laugh?* You guessed it! I told my family and they believed me. And now, I'm telling the world. When Jesus heals, consider it done. Don't let the evil one confuse you into thinking that you are not healed. "Jesus personally carried the load of our sins in His own body when He died on the cross, so that we can be finished with sin and live a good life from now on. For His wounds have healed ours!" 1 Peter 2:24. (Reach Out.) Although this verse refers to our spiritual wounds, we can take it to mean our physical wounds also, because Matthew, Chapter 8 verse 17 says, "This fulfilled the prophecy of Isaiah, 'He took our sickness and bore our diseases.' " (Reach Out.)

When our vacation was over, we returned home. Cindy had seen a difference in me before vacation. Instead of pain-filled evenings, there was reading the Bible—fellowship with her, and instead of moans and groans, there were smiles, extra patience, and a more peaceful atmosphere. But, after our vacation, she noticed an even bigger difference. For the first time in her life, when she came home from a date, I was in bed, not waiting up for her, yelling that it was too late for her to be out, and nagging at her, asking her where she had been. She wondered why I wasn't worrying about her being out anymore. She was glad about all these changes.

I answered, "I have put you in the Lord's hands. He can take care of you at all times. I've given you to the Lord and placed my trust in Him."

After that, she started to ask questions and shared with me the fact that she too had been studying her Bible and listening to my sister and I talk about the Lord these last few weeks. I asked her if she would like to go to church with me the following Saturday night, because we were having a special program, and Hank was coming home from Bible school that weekend, and we were all looking forward to seeing him. My heart yearned for her to go; I knew it would be a spirit-filled service and she would enjoy it. She said that she'd have to think about it and she'd let me know later.

On Friday night, when Hank arrived, he brought with him three fellow students and the instant that we met them, we loved them. After all, we were brothers and sisters in the Lord. Saturday, my sister spent the afternoon with us and asked Cindy to go along with us to church that night. Cindy surprised me by saying yes.

The special program that evening consisted of a trio called "The First Revelation," a group that has dedicated its lives to the work of the Lord, and have brought many people to meet Jesus Christ through their music and inspirational singing. The Spirit of the Lord just filled the church that night. You knew that Jesus was there. When the altar call came, praise God, Bud took my hand and said, "Will you go up there with me?"

Would I? Try to stop me!

Then my joy overflowed, when right behind us, our daughter came up to the altar. Our gift from God was going up to accept Jesus. Oh, the love and thanks were and still are too much for mere words. There were many happy tears that evening. Praise the Lord!

Sunday was spent in love and sharing with our guests and family. Here again, the Lord showed me that He was at work in my life. I prepared a meal and served sixteen people. Normally, this amount of company in our little house would have driven me right up the proverbial wall, but my stomach did not even get butterflies. I never hit the panic button. Me, who had never liked having people around and would never cook for anyone, loved every minute of it, and to this day, I delight in having my house overflow.

Chapter Nine

In the past year, my husband's health had not been too good. He was having troubles and was to go back to the doctor on Tuesday for possible surgery. I went to my mother's to say good-bye to our new friends. We shared the joy of Bud's and Cindy's salvation, and then I spoke to them of my concern for Bud's health and possible surgery.

There was the chair in the middle of the kitchen again. Only, this time, I couldn't wait to sit in it. I was to be a proxy for Bud.

We all started to pray for Bud, asking for his health and, please no surgery. The Holy Spirit so filled that room that even one who had never believed before could have felt it. When the Spirit of the Lord is present there is such a feeling of love abounding in everyone, that you actually feel your heart swelling to the bursting point, the joy is more than you can bear without laughing, crying and dancing. The very air you are breathing seems to have the fragrance of Heaven.

As we prayed, I felt such a burning sensation start in my head, which quickly spread through my entire body and out through my feet. It was uncomfortable and I was glad to have it leave as quickly as it had come. But, it had left such a thanksgiving in its place, that I couldn't wait to tell Bud because I knew it was a healing surge that I had felt from our Lord and since I was Bud's proxy, I felt Bud had been healed.

When he went to the doctor's the next day, it was found that the trouble was healed. No surgery. But it seemed that the gout, kidney infection and high blood pressure were still there. I had known such a surge of healing flow through me, I didn't understand why Bud wasn't completely healed.

We both prayed about this. Was Bud's faith strong enough? We felt that it was. You see, we know that Jesus never lies and there had been a healing. We asked ourselves, "Was Bud not believing, was he having doubts? Help us," we prayed. "Show us Your will Lord."

The Lord answered. He told Bud and I that *I* had been healed. A miracle! Praise God, not just my arm, everything!

Ulcer—gone!

Headache—gone, no bruise on the skull!

Legs—fine, no more spasms!

Allergies—gone!

I can eat eggs, pork anything that I thank God for. He blesses me to eat. My nerves are like steel. No jumping at every little sound, no trembling of the fingers. No more gas in the chest. After surgery the spleen had torn, and caused intense gas pressure in my chest. Not now! I work, keep house, enjoy company and if I even feel tired from a long day's work, I say, "Thank you Jesus for the strength you have given me." Power surges through my strong healthy body.

I can honestly always say that I feel great. Bud was so happy. He thanked Jesus and thanked Him every day for my healing, for he had asked many times over the years for me to be healed.

Those first two weeks after Bud and Cindy accepted Jesus were full of love and sharing and happiness. But then things began to change between Bud and I.

After 26 years of near perfect marriage, we were at

each other's throats. We were fighting about our belief and faith in Jesus. We didn't see eye to eye on anything. I knew that my husband was saved. *Must be me*, I thought.

If we read the Bible together, we each had a different explanation and I accused Bud of being a fanatic. He accused me of trying to turn him from Jesus Christ. Oh, the hell that the evil one puts us through. We, who had never argued much, in 26 years, were shouting terrible hurting things at each other. We both spent days praying, reading the Bible and fighting. I was convinced that I wasn't saved. You see, sometimes the devil tricks us into thinking that we aren't really saved. One thing I have to say is that when you meet Jesus you also become aware of the devil, because the Holy Spirit is now showing you where you fall down, and just how the old evil one gets to you. Praise the Lord for victory over this though.

The third day, the Lord just seemed to say one name to me over and over again. Nancy. Nancy. Well, I went to her house. She wasn't there, still I kept hearing in my head, "Find Nancy, find Nancy." I went to another Christian's home and she tracked down Nancy. I have to tell you that she was one of the folks in the Bible study that I had not gotten along with. Now I loved her as a sister and I needed her! When the Spirit of the Lord is in you and in another person, there is a love bond and understanding between you that cannot be explained.

So here was proud Alice, telling Nancy of her troubles and fears. God has, and will continue to bless Nancy. She prayed, asking the Lord to guide her to help me, and He did, and she did! I left feeling calm and sure of my salvation. Now Bud and I had to talk and pray. He was going to leave that morning. We just couldn't stay together. When I left Nancy's house, I returned home and asked Bud to pray once more, and to take it all to Jesus, and I would do the same. I wish that I could say that our troubles left us at once, but they didn't. Yet, as our faith grew and we read and prayed together, we began to realize that it was not God's will for us to be like this, but the devil was trying to turn us away from God. But there is nothing to fear, Jesus never leaves you. We made it. With God's help, we put the evil one aside, and at this writing, our love for each other is deeper than ever.

Chapter Ten

I will try here to make clear my feelings about the Holy Spirit. It is the Spirit of the Living Lord Jesus Christ. When you truly believe in Jesus, and invite Him into your heart, you have a small part of Jesus' Spirit in you. Jesus never hated anyone. Jesus loved all. Jesus never held spite. Jesus forgave all. Jesus was never mean or unkind. He was always gentle.

So, when you have Jesus dwelling in you, how can you hate? The Holy Spirit opens your eyes to the inner people, not the color, not the nationality, not the religion. The Holy Spirit lets you see people as the Lord sees them, and that's with the utmost love and compassion. The Lord wants us all. We are a part of the Lord, thus we cannot hate another part of the Lord. His Holy Spirit helps in guiding you in all things. Galatians 5:22–23 says, "But the fruit of the Spirit is love, joy peace, longsuffering, gentleness, goodness and faith, meekness temperance—against such there is no law." (King James.)

The closer that you get to Jesus, the more you try to serve Him, the more the evil of this word tries to get to you by using your weakest points. We all have weak points and always will, but if you put complete trust in Jesus and turn to Him for everything, big or small, the evil cannot turn you away. Several times my feet have started to cramp. The first time I started for my pills, the strong thought came to me (from the Lord) that "you are healed." I turned, and moved away from the cupboard where the pills were kept, and the second that I turned, the pain left me. Always remember and say to yourself, "Greater is He that is in me, than he who is in the world." The evil in the world is indeed powerful, but the Lord is much more powerful and when you have the Lord, you have the power to put evil down. Thank you Jesus!

By the grace of God I was healed. By the grace of God I will stay healed. His will be done; not mine.

There is so much that I could tell about Bud and Cindy's walk with Jesus, but that is their testimony, and I am telling only what parts affected my testimony. But it has changed their lives, and as reborn Christians, they have received great blessings and are joyfully serving our Lord in all ways.

Did I keep the sureness that I was saved? No. I think that all new Christians go through this. I knew that the Holy Spirit was growing inside. My faith most of the time was stronger, but then, I'd hear someone with a different point of view and off I'd go again, "I'm not saved. I'm not serving the Lord. I'm not worthy enough." I started to read and pray more. I started asking more questions, and began to "want all." The final step (or so I thought) was to be baptized with the Holy Spirit, or as some say, Holy Ghost. Why? I wanted to know once and for all that I was saved. I was on my way to eternal life, I knew that I was spiritually weak. I'd never make it on my own. I would falter, and, without the guidance and fullness of the Holy Spirit, I would maybe slip back. Besides, I wanted to know Jesus just as much as a human being could. In other words, I was ready to fully commit myself to Him. I belonged, heart and soul to our Lord. I wanted to serve Him in all ways, and being so weak, without the Holy Spirit dwelling within in full power, I'd never make it. But how to get it? Was I sure that I wanted it? I knew that I didn't really want to speak in tongues, I just wanted the fulfillment it promised. I wasn't really sure that I could handle the gifts that God would give to those who served Him. How little did I know, for Jesus said, "Come to me and I will give you rest, all of you who work so hard beneath a heavy yoke. Wear my yoke for it fits perfectly, and let me teach you for I am gentle and humble and you shall find rest for yourselves, for I give you only light burdens." Matthew 11:28–30 (Living Bible). You see, in this, Jesus is trying to tell us to let Him do it. He will take care of everything, and He knows just what we can and cannot do.

Yet, I was a little afraid. This baptism of the Holy Spirit was something I couldn't completely understand. For several weeks, I asked Christians, "What, how, why, when?" I wondered if you really felt closer to God. Yes, I believed you would feel closer to God. After all, this was the whole purpose. Why was I fearful? It would be a supernatural experience and anything we humans cannot explain we are usually afraid of. I had studied the Scriptures enough to know that speaking in a different language could be a part of it. Did I want this gift? I was unsure. Also, it meant a complete giving of yourself to the Lord. I would not control my life anymore, the Lord would.

I would receive power and gifts from God. Could I handle this? But, more would be expected of me—was I ready? *I'm not worthy of this*, I said to myself. Of course not, it's a gift.

For weeks I prayed, sometimes asking for the Baptism of the Holy Spirit, sometimes saying, "I'm not ready Lord." I was deeply confused and our Lord knew this. God is a God of order—not confusion; so it was best to pray and study more.

Meanwhile, Christmas was approaching. We could hardly wait. Our first birthday in Christ. Cindy wanted a real tree, nothing could be fake this year. She and Bud went to the woods at our church and cut down a tree that filled one fourth of our small living room. The love and fellowship that was in our home was perfect. Every night, as Bud and I knelt together in prayer, our hearts overflowed in thanks to Jesus. We had extra special blessings that year. Just one of the many blessings were the love and fellowship of three fine young Christian men, Mark, Bubby and Wally, who visited three or four times a week. As we praised our Lord and sang praise songs, our hearts were filled. Hank, Mark, Bubby and Wally were to spend Christmas day with us. It was to be a very special day.

Cindy was dating a fine young Jewish boy and asked if she could invite him for Christmas. "Yes, of course," I said. "But it will be a day of our Lord. Be sure that he is aware that there will be a full house of Christians." Praise the Lord, he accepted.

Our Lord's birthday was perfect. Love was overflowing and not only did our welcomed Jewish friend come for dinner, but joined in with Bud in playing his guitar and singing right with us. He felt the love in our midst and stayed all day.

Our New Year's was also a joy to our hearts. It was not the usual kind of New Year's celebration that the world offers. But it was an invitation from Nancy and her husband John to attend a Christian Spirit filled New Year's evening. We spent the night in songs of praise, and laughter filled our throats and love filled our hearts. I pray that all of our New Years may be the same.

Chapter Eleven

Shortly after New Year's and after an unusual praise service at our church, Hank (home for the weekend), two other Christian students, plus Mark, Bubby and Wally, my mother and sister came to our house. We had refreshments and fellowship for a short time, when the visiting student with Hank, having received a special message from the Lord, suddenly looked at me and asked, "Do you believe you can be baptized in the Holy Spirit?"

I answered, "Yes, why yes."

Suddenly the room was different. A hush had fallen, and yet it seemed that no outside noises could be heard. I felt as though that room was suspended in time. Phil then broke the silence and asked, "Do you believe that you can receive this gift right now?"

The room was still hushed. All eyes were on me. For many months I had prayed about this, now was the time, a decision had to be made. *Did I really believe?* I asked myself. *Yes truly*—did I want this total commitment? *Yes with all my heart.* Was I ready? All these thoughts went through my mind in a few seconds.

I answered Phil simply, "Yes, but I do not want to speak in tongues."

Phil bent his head and replied, "Let's all pray." I interrupted him. "Don't you want me in the center of the room so that you can lay hands on me."

"That's not necessary," he said. "We will all stay just where we are."

I bowed my head. I felt the presence of the Lord there in my living room. I heard only a few words, "Dear Lord, we ask you now for the Baptism of the Holy Spirit for Alice." I heard no more of any sound or prayer after that.

It was as if just the Lord and I were talking. The Lord said to get on my knees, but I kept thinking that I was supposed to stay right where I was. Suddenly, with no action on my part, I was gently lifted from the couch where I was sitting, and my knees landed as softly as a leaf in the center of the room. He told me, oh praise God, I was going to receive this special gift!

It was just Jesus and I in all time and space. The biggest, most holy temple could not have been filled with my Lord's presence any more than my living room. I said, "Oh thank you, Lord. Thank you!" Then I felt a gurgling sensation coming up my throat and I turned the word into "Hallelujah." Then I received the full power. I was filled with the Holy Spirit. I overflowed. I was like a fountain. My body could not contain all this Spirit; it flowed through every pore. My body felt as light as a piece of down, and I felt that I could float. I was pure and clean. All sin was wiped out of my heart. I was a child of God, sister to Jesus Christ now, and forever more. I was complete as a person as I had never been. Joy, great love and peace flowed through me, around me and back into my very soul. I knew that I was in the presence of something very holy. A mere "Thank you, Jesus" was not enough. A beautiful onslaught of words, in a language I have never heard before, flowed from my lips. The words followed each other so smoothly and sounded so beautiful that I just wanted to go on and on praising the Lord in this glorious new way. I realized that I had full control of these beautiful words. I could continue to talk to my Lord or I could stop anytime I wanted. Oh, how I praised Him!

Slowly, I became aware of the others in the room. I heard my mother crying. Bud, too, was weeping and praising the Lord. Praising Jesus. Soft prayers of, "Thank you, Jesus. Praise you, Jesus. Hallelujah Jesus," filled the room. I stopped speaking and opened my eyes. There was a glow in that room. I looked at Bud, his face glowed, it really glowed! Tears ran down his cheeks. His hands were raised to Heaven, as he continued to pray. My mother was sobbing quietly as she prayed. Everyone continued to pray softly to the Lord. I looked up into my sister's face and she smiled at me and the love on her face almost blinded me. For the first time in my life, I was speechless. I sat back up on the couch besides Wally. He and I just sat looking at each other.

What were my thoughts? None really. I was in awe. You don't come so close to our Lord and not be in complete awe. But, happiness is such a little word compared to what I felt. I could not have explained it then, nor can I explain it now. Everyone was so happy. They shared my deep joy. As Hank said, the Lord's Spirit had been so thick, he could have sliced it. You see, there is a different feeling and fragrance when the Lord is present.

Since it was very late and we were all so filled with the presence of the Lord (I think that each of us wanted to go pray and be with the Lord), everyone soon went home. Bud and I said goodnight to our dear friends and then Bud opened up his arms and I just walked into them and again, we felt our Lord's presence. After twenty-seven years of marriage, in that one moment, we really were one.

As we knelt at the bed, we were too full of the Spirit to pray. We just smiled and said, "Thank you, thank you, thank you." Did I sleep? No. I was too happy to sleep, and yet never have I felt so rested. It seemed as if I had slept at least 10 hours.

Have I changed? Completely. Some of the most obvious changes are a great love for Scripture. I just can't read my Bible enough, and I have a deeper, more complete understanding of Scripture.

I also have a deep feeling of inner confidence, of inner wellbeing. No matter what trials are on the outside piling up, a closer communication with my Lord will stay with me. I follow my will—praying that if it is not the will of the Lord, that He will let me know. He does. I feel like one with everything belonging to our Lord, past—present—future.

I find myself praising the Lord dozens of times a day, and the more I praise Him, the better I feel. Blessings seem to flow down on top of me. My faith seems to grow stronger, and I pray that if a really big test comes along, my faith will be there, full grown and rock steady.

Is the baptism necessary for salvation? No. Should everyone seek it? Yes. Of course, this is between each one and their walk with the Lord. For me it seemed a must. The baptism of the Holy Spirit brings one much closer to the Lord and should be sought after by everyone.

Is it something to fear? No, indeed. How can anyone fear a Lord so full of love? If anyone should ask me, "Should I seek it?" I would have to answer yes.

Do I ever doubt my salvation now? No, never. But don't ever think that this is the answer to eternal salvation. It is not. We must pray and study the Scriptures daily.

I like to think that many years ago my grandmother planted a seed, and each of my steps closer to Jesus brings that seed nearer to becoming a beautiful flower that will someday bloom in Heaven. I was asked recently, "Do I believe in Heaven?"

Yes, truly, with all my heart.

Chapter Twelve

For three years we have had the ugliest, dearest little fluffy dog who is indeed part of the family. We all adore her. Now, this little dog had never seen anyone in our house but my mother and sister. She was terrified if strangers came in. Well, all at once our home was filled with laughing, loud strangers. The first time, she ran in terror, barking at everything. As usual, these evenings ended in a prayer circle. After the first evening, we all came to realize that no matter where she was in the house, the second that we got in a circle, she came and sat right in the middle, until we said Amen. Then she would leave. After watching her do this for months, we decided, even animals sense love and want to be part of it. I write about our little Buffy because she is a big part of my testimony. We laughingly call her our "Holy Dog." We know that she senses the great love in our midst.

    One day in mid-winter I noticed that Buffy seemed to grow more and more listless. You'd have to know how playful and frisky she usually is to notice that she was ill. Before Christmas, I had noticed a small lump on the inside of her leg, but thinking that it was nothing, I didn't keep track of it. But, a month later, I realized that she didn't want to jump anymore; even getting into the car, she would fall, and didn't seem to be able to control her back legs. I was very concerned.

One day, while sitting on the couch reading my Bible, I noticed that she had large lumps on the inside of each leg. I instantly asked the Lord to let her be alright, but I felt that perhaps it wouldn't be right to lay hands or pray for a dog. (Dumb of me—see, I'm still learning.)

I took her to the vet the next day, and after his examination of her, he said that she had a very large hernia on each side of her female organs. If he were to operate, she might never walk again, so he advised me to keep a close watch on her because their growth could burst her bowels. So, if we saw them growing, we were to bring her in for surgery, at once. We were a sad little family that Wednesday night. We dearly loved that little dog.

A few days later, same couch, same thing: me reading my Bible, Buffy on her back beside me. I was reading of Christ on His way to the cross, not thinking of anything but what I was reading, when all at once I knew that Jesus just loved all and everything that He had created, and if our little Buffy had been at the cross that day, as full of love as she is, she would have followed Him. I found myself crying and holding her up, telling her it was OK, that Jesus loved her, too. I could see in my mind, our Saviour dragging His cross up that hill, followed by that scraggly little dog. (Do I sound insane? If so, please let me be.)

I could feel the love all around that little dog and me. I laid her back down, placed a hand on each lump and thanked Jesus for His love of her and for healing her. She seemed almost to know what I was saying. I know that she felt the great love around us. She didn't even attempt to move, just looked at me with those big eyes full of love and trust.

I went back to reading, feeling so happy. You see, when the Lord really talked to me there was no doubt in my mind that she was healed. A few days later, as she ran and played, my husband was watching her and commented that she seemed better. I answered, "She's healed. See for yourself."

I turned her over. No hernia. Bud just looked at me, so I repeated what I've just written. Buffy is fine now, she jumps and plays again. If you are going to the car, watch out because when that car door opens, she is coming in!

You may ask, why a chapter on a dog when there is such need in the world, such hunger, and war? Don't you see? The great love and mercy flowing from the Lord is for everyone and everything that he has created. He cares. If we would all turn to Him and have His Spirit guiding us there would be no more hunger, war, need, hate or prejudice. The world would be full of love and sharing with each other. With the Lord at the head, whether it be a little family like ours, or the whole world, there would be peace, love, trust, mercy, healing, strength and joy. We could have all this with the Lord in charge of this world. It could be a Heaven on earth.

GOD IS IN CONTROL

In all things, large or small, know that God is in control. I'm kind of hardheaded, and sometimes I don't always learn the lesson easily. In the early spring I set about rebuilding my front flower bed. I needed some large rocks which I found across the road in the high grass. My constant companion, Buffy, loved these little trips into new territory, and since I had her on a long rope, she could run fairly free. I had balanced three very large rocks on my arm, when I realized that there was a car coming and Buffy had run dangerously near the road. In my concern for her safety, I forgot I was balancing three rocks and as I pulled her back, the biggest rock fell out of my arm and landed with a "squash" on my right foot. Oh, the pain. *Oh, dear Jesus*, I prayed, *please take it away.*

I limped to the house, brought Buffy in and sat down to pray. I believed it would be healed right away. I have received many, many miracles, so why not this time, too?

I laid my hands on it and claimed healing by His stripes. It still hurt, worse than ever. In the next few hours, Bud and I prayed for the healing power of Our Lord. My foot got worse. It turned all colors, and was so swollen, not even a slipper would fit. So, off to the hospital we went. X rays were taken, and the usual routine examination made. The only relief that the doctor could offer was a crutch and some pain pills, as it was smashed all the way to the bone and he said that it would take weeks to heal.

In great pain, trying not to cry, I rode home from the hospital with Bud. There, too, I had been unable to get relief. Oh, Lord, what was I to do?

Bud, in his quiet voice, glanced at me and asked, "Did you thank the Lord for this?"

I was speechless. After a few more miles, almost home, I answered, "I will not thank the Lord for what the devil did!" End of discussion.

When we arrived home, I packed my foot in ice and tried everything to ease the pain. When I tried to go to bed, it hurt. If I sat and kept it still, it hurt. Nothing could ease the pain. "Oh, Lord," I said. "I don't know why you wanted this to happen, but thank you anyway. I know you want me to learn something from all this, so I thank you." Breathing the Amen, I fell asleep.

Being a slow riser, I'm not too alert in the morning. When it was time to get up in my usual half-awake state, I swung my feet out of bed, searched for my slippers with my feet when suddenly I was wide awake. *I have a smashed foot*, I thought. I looked down. Both feet were the same size. Both the same color. I bent my foot—arched my foot—nothing, no pain. I tried to bend my toes, a little twinge, but not much. I suppose it was just a token to remind me a little of the great pain a few hours ago. Why? What was the last thing I remembered? Yes, I had thanked the Lord for the pain. Of course, He was showing me that He is in control of all things at all times—don't give any credit to the devil for even the hard times, for God is in control even of the devil. Praise the Lord!

Having learned my lesson, God healed my foot at once. "For God sometimes uses sorrow in our lives to help us turn away from sin and seek eternal life. We should never regret his sending it. But the sorrow of the man who is not a Christian is not the sorrow of true repentance and does not prevent eternal death." II Corinthians 7:10 (See also, I Peter 5:10.) For He said, praise me in all things and I will bless you.

Chapter Thirteen

MIRACLES EVERY DAY!!!

I know God has been so great and good to me that I have to share it, and since I can't afford to travel around, this book will travel for me. Mark 5:19 says, "Go home to your friends, and tell them what wonderful things God has done for you; and how merciful he has been." God will be good to you; your life will be changed. Many books have been written by great people on miracles, such as those by Pat Boone, Oral Roberts, Billy Graham and others. All are true. You might think, why sure, they receive miracles, but they're great and godly men, none of them are like me. Well, I'm like you. I have a salary range under $8,000, and I live on a budget. Yes, I'm like you. But, I'm also like those godly men, too. God plays no favorites. (See Ephesians 6:9.) I receive, look for, and expect miracles every day.

To list a few of the big miracles we have had, there are: my healing, Buffy's healing, and my smashed foot. But the sweetest ones are the every-day kind: the quick and needed ones. You may be feeling a little down and ask the Lord to help you and suddenly the phone rings and a voice says, "Praise the Lord, how are you today?" and you answer, "Praise the Lord, I'm fine." And suddenly, you *are* fine. The voice may be a friend you know only slightly, and she may say, "I don't know why, but the Lord seemed to say, 'call Alice.' " Then we laugh and talk about how great He is. He takes care of his own.

Coincidence? Try this:

We had planned to go to Pennsylvania for a long weekend. Our beloved aunts, uncles and Bud's family were all living there and we hoped to share our great joy and salvation with them and enjoy being with all the people we love so much. Well, I came home from a Stanley demonstration (I'm a demonstrator part-time to help out with the finances), and my daughter told me that the washing machine was broken.

Boy, was it ever! It sounded like a Mack truck stuck in the mud. It wouldn't bring the water in, just sat there and made noise. I greeted Bud at the door with the news that the washing machine is broken, there goes our trip. We didn't have money to pay for both. Well, he worked on it and tried just about everything, when the Lord spoke to me. Why that machine and everything that we have belongs to the Lord. Why can't I just thank Him for fixing it, and forget it?

Bud was still in the process of trying to make the machine work, when I told him that the Lord would fix it, we were going to Pennsylvania. Big loving Bud just gave me his grin and said Jesus was a carpenter, not a repair man. You see, we had always before, believed the quote, "The Lord helps them that help themselves." Wrong. The Lord helps them that can't help themselves. I had to go out for a meeting, so I left, feeling sure that the machine was OK.

When I returned, Bud met me at the door with a sheepish grin and said, "I did two loads of laundry."

I said, "What was wrong with it?"

He answered, "I don't know. I didn't do a thing to it; but when you left, I pushed the knob and it worked! It runs quieter than ever and I stopped and started it

over and over; there's nothing wrong with it."
 Did you guess my answer. "That Jesus is some repair man, isn't he?"

Do you want a few more miracles? I could fill pages with them. Last winter, on a very icy driveway, I lost control of my car. It was sliding very quickly, sideways into a building, and the wheel in my hands was useless. I caught a glimpse of the door of the building, just inches away from the right side of the car and coming up fast. I said, "Lord drive this car." At once, as if a giant hand had hold on it, the car went forward, and drove off the ice. There were about six people watching all this, and a week or so later, one of them asked how the car straightened out so fast. My answer, "The Lord was driving."
 Before Christmas last year, I wanted to send a love gift to my special friends at Pine Crest Bible School. I made cookies and other goodies, and took the box to the post office and mailed it. When I came home, Cindy asked where the fudge was that I had made the night before. I explained who it was for, and that I would make her some that evening.
 When I got out the fudge mix and was reading the directions, I suddenly realized that I had, in my haste the night before, switched the ingredients. The recipe called for two cups of sugar and half cup of butter, and I had inverted the measurements. Two cups of butter and a half cup of sugar. I felt badly because the fudge would not be fit to eat and they did not get home-made goodies at school and that box would have been such a treat to them. I took it to my Lord. I asked him to handle that little mistake and to fix up those two pans of fudge. Then I forgot about it, knowing that he could and would do this for his own. A few weeks later I found out that the box had arrived in A-1 condition and

that the fudge was delicious and they really enjoyed it. Am I the only one in the family that enjoys miracles? No. Read on.

Cindy has a tiny little car. She works days and is taking night courses for a degree in business. She has to travel on a big interstate highway every day and of course at 5:00 P.M. the traffic is congested. She came in one night, white and shaken and told us this story. She had been driving at about 50 MPH when a car coming off the "in" ramp pulled in front of the tractor-trailer in front of her. The trucker hit his air brakes and Cindy tried to stop her little car. She couldn't. Her front end was going in under the truck. She knew that she was going to be smashed. She didn't tell us what she cried out, it doesn't matter, but as she was telling us, her face changed and a look of wonder radiated from her eyes. Her voice, which had been high-pitched, bordering on the edge of hysteria, became strangely quiet as she said, "My car was going in under the truck, when all at once, it wasn't. The truck was ahead of me and nothing was happening. The traffic was moving away." She went to her room while her dad and I thanked Jesus.

Do you take Jesus to work with you? Bud can tell you that he does. Bud is a custodian at an elementary school and some days that can be a real test. Many times during the day, he asks for patience and strength, but one rather hectic day, hard at work, with just an hour before quitting time, Bud realized that he had lost his keys. They normally were on a key ring on his belt, and he has to use these keys all day long, and he could not finish his work without them. He hunted everywhere; over and over he checked the halls. No keys. What to do? For a Christian there's only one answer: ask Jesus.

He stopped searching and asked Jesus in prayer to help him find those keys. Jesus told him that they had fallen in the garbage bag. Now, Bud knew that was unlikely, but he never questions the Lord, so straight to the garbage he went. Guess what he found there? Pocketing the keys, he returned to his duties, finished his work, and praised the Lord.

I could write a book on miracles alone. But I've tried to recap just some of the miracles in our every day lives to tell you in all things big or small, the Lord is there. Just reach out and take your miracles. Don't let them pass you by.

Can Jesus perform miracles? If you doubt, try looking up some of these Bible passages in the book of John. John 2:11, John 4:50–54, John 5:8, John 6:19–20, John 11:42–44, John 14:12–13. Does Jesus still perform miracles? He sure does! See Hebrews, Chapter 13, verse 8: "Jesus Christ is the same yesterday, today and forever." Praise God! In no uncertain terms, He is telling us to grab on to those miracles just as the apostles did, and the people of Jesus' day that he healed when he walked the earth. And, in the future, when times get rougher, those miracles will still be at our disposal. All we have to do is walk in the realm of God's love and let the miracles pour down on us from heaven.

Chapter Fourteen

REWARDS!!!

Most of my life has been lonely and insecure. How is my life now? To answer that, all I need is one verse of scripture—*Living Bible*, Ephesians 2:19 "I am a member of God's family. I am a citizen in his country. I belong in God's household."

Insecure? No, not when I know who I am. Ephesians 1:3–10 is such a beautiful passage that I must include all of it here, forgive me for the length. (Reach Out.) "How we praise God, the Father of our Lord Jesus Christ, who has blessed us with every blessing in heaven because we belong to Christ. Long ago, even before He made the world, God chose us to be His very own, through what Christ would do for us; He decided then to make us holy in His eyes, without a single fault—we who stand before Him covered with His love. His unchanging plan has always been to adopt us into His own family by sending Jesus Christ to die for us. And He did this because He wanted to! Now all praise to God for His wonderful kindness to us and His favor that He has poured out upon us that He took away all our sins through the blood of His Son, by whom we are saved; And He has showered down upon us the richness of His grace-for how well He understands us and knows what is best for us at all times. God has told us His secret reason for sending Christ, a plan He decided on in mercy long ago; And this was His purpose: that when the time is ripe He will gather us all together from wherever we are—in heaven or on earth—to be with Him in Christ, forever." See also Ephesians 1:14.

Could anyone feel lonely with a promise like that with them? The joys of serving Christ are endless. We have a happy, active, full life. There is no time to be lonely or bored. We go to Bible study every Friday night. How boring, you may think. Well, please believe me that the love and fellowship we have together as we sing, praise God, laugh and pray together is in no way boring. Sharing with people something as deep as your personal experiences with our Lord is a wonderful feeling. Common bonds are developed, and one tends to no longer lack faith in the human race. Just think, with all the different people in the world, all the good and the bad, there is still one and only one common denominator: God. Loneliness vanishes with God holding us together.

Sometimes, we drop in on the Monday night Bible study—again a night filled to overflowing with love. They are truly a precious group of Christians. We're the last to leave church on Sunday. Why this ex-lonely woman can't find enough time to talk with all the loving people headed her way.

Sunday night usually finds us at a praise service, sometimes at our church, sometimes with a different church group. I should explain here that a praise service is one in which you simply praise the Lord. You come to the service with that in mind. It is not a healing service, although sometimes people are healed. It is not a regular service, with the regular hell-fire-and-brimstone sermons, it is merely a specific service meant to praise God and to thank Him for all the blessings He has sent our way. By praising the Lord, you are also doing yourself a big favor. You are, first of all, obeying a direct command of the Lord. "Rejoice in the Lord always: and again I say, Rejoice." Philippians 4:4 (King James). "Always be full of joy in the Lord; I say it again, rejoice." Philippians 4:4. (Reach Out.) This statement is so full of power that you have to put it into practice to actually see how it works. The Holy Spirit is telling us here to praise the Lord, be happy in the Lord, and He says it *twice*: "*again* I say rejoice." Praise God! By thanking our Father in heaven for all His gifts, we are making way for more gifts to be showered down on us, and we truly learn just where our blessings come from. There is so much love at one of these praise services that sometimes friends come home with us for more fellowship.

And still the blessings continue to come. Through my work as a Stanley dealer, I met a group of young people, all serving the Lord. They have brought me more joy than I can tell. I'm invited to their homes for parties, and I learn from them and I love them all so much. I met the girl who is typing this book there and we spend hours talking and laughing and praising the Lord. I have met some of their parents, and usually one of our Stanley parties turns into another group discussion about the Lord. Being with a different age group has taught me many things. These kids are taking the Lord on his promises and sometimes have trouble convincing their parents that they are doing the right thing. Here I have been able to help and praise God, to show, one mother especially, how real Jesus is and how He can help now, with every day problems. I love them all so much, and I know that they love me too. We are all sisters in Christ.

I found myself volunteering for church work. Right now, I am chairman of the annual church fair. Me, who at one time had all she could do to take care of her own family, now I am taking on all kinds of extra responsibilities, and, praise God, I love it! All I can see is more good times in Jesus, more love, all coming my way.

Bud, who was blessed with a good voice and talent to play the guitar, sometimes sings and plays for the Lord at different places. Don't think, "How nice of him." Believe me, the good times we have had with all these new friends is so important that playing for the Lord is a privilege, and Bud is happy to do it.

My sister and Mark decided to learn to play the guitar. They prayed and pledged their playing to the Lord and both are playing beautifully now. But, here again our home is filled with love, laughter, and fellowship as we gather each week for Bud to teach them their lesson. Those evenings are priceless.

Needless to say, I do a lot of baking. Cakes are my favorite, and I have never enjoyed anything as much as opening my home to all or any who will bless us by coming to visit and sharing one of my lopsided cakes. When you walk with the Lord, doing things for people becomes a blessing instead of being a "drag."

Before I met Jesus, whenever I had a bad day, and was uptight, bored, or just plain miserable, poor Bud had his ear bent all evening, about how rotten the day had been to me. He must have become mighty tired of all of it. Well, I still bend his ear every night, and he loves it! Now I have good things to tell him. Someone called with great news that they wanted to share, or where we're going that night, I even tell him about people who have called to perhaps just have me pray with them. My life is so full now. I love it. Praise you, Jesus!

Do I keep a spotless house as I used to? No way!

But, if you walk into our home, you won't mind the dust on the furniture, or you won't notice that the floor needs vacuuming, because in our home, Jesus lives, and loves and anyone can feel it. Who minds a little dust, if Jesus can be found in our home?

Have you followed my walk with the Lord these past few months? Have you seen the hundreds of loving people I've met, sang with, praised the Lord with and prayed with? Am I lonely, bored, tired? Not me. Not Bud or Cindy. I Corinthians, Chapter 13, verse 13 speaks of the three things that will still be here when all else is gone. What a reassurance to hear . . . "There are three things that remain—faith, hope, and love—and the greatest of these is love." Read I Corinthians 13. The whole chapter explains just what love is, in God's eyes, and gives hope and faith to anyone who reads it.

Chapter Fifteen

GIFTS!!!!

When you hear a sermon or discussion on the "Church" you may think of it meaning a particular denomination; however, after accepting the Lord, and studying your Bible, you learn that the church as Christ means it, is everyone who proclaims Him Lord. We are His Church. We are His body and since the body has many different parts, even within the body of Christ, we are all different, yet we need one another.

Jesus gives His church "gifts" so that it may grow and thrive. Read I Corinthians 12. In the months following my baptism, my gifts were slowly starting to show. As I stated, my part-time job involves meeting people, sometimes as many as 100 per week. Therefore, I do not, cannot remember even one quarter of those I meet. So, in January when a young lady came to my door with orders for Stanley, I not only didn't know her, but couldn't even remember where or when I met her, and yet the strangest thing happened. As she reminded me, she was Kate, and as she walked up to me I suddenly knew that she was full of the Spirit of the Lord. I wanted to hug her, and when she left, I told Bud, "There goes a Spirit-filled Christian."

He said, "How did you know that?"

I answered, "I don't know how I know, I just know!"

I pondered on this. How did I know? Was it a guess? Was it true? In a few weeks I again met Kate at a party. I didn't remember her again, but still, I knew that Kate was full of the Lord, and not only her but several others there were also Spirit-filled. I didn't know that this was a special gift, I just enjoyed it. Then I began to realize that even strangers, people walking into a room were full of the Spirit of the Lord and I loved them. What a lovely feeling. As the months went by, I realized that I not only knew at times people were Spirit-filled, but I also got a different wave length. I sensed a depth or overflowing more so in some than others. Finally it dawned on me one day, that, Praise the Lord, this was a gift.

As I've mentioned before, I have a great love for scripture. I've never read anything so thrilling, so interesting, so compelling, in all of my life. I couldn't find enough time to really enjoy my Bible as I would have liked to. Hours flew by and still I hated to lay it down. Bud would ask me a question, I'd open my Bible and it seemed so simple, why hadn't he understood?

My friends, family, and the people at Bible study would discuss the Bible and I'd get so impatient with them. Why didn't they understand what was read? Didn't they read their Bibles as much as I did? It was so interesting and so informative to me that every verse has a powerful message. Why, one verse, any verse, could be discussed for hours. Didn't they see that? Why didn't they understand? Was I reading more into it than was actually there? Why did they read a verse and just seem to say, "Yes, that's the way it reads," and I would read the same verse and see, Wow—the depth, the inner meaning. It really said so much more. Should I try and not see all of this? I tried. People told me, "Take the Bible literally, there is no other meaning than what it says."

Fine. It says Jesus is the door, now, let's see. If you can take that literally, He is the door to eternal life. But, you just can't take that sentence literally. There is so much more than that. I began to wonder. Was this also a gift? Is that why, in a discussion, I always seemed to get more out of scripture than others? I prayed about it and accepted this gift with the greatest—greatest of joy!

What other gifts do I have? I don't know. You see, as I grow in the body of Christ, I'm sure He will give me as many as are necessary to help His church. He will guide me as to where, how and when these gifts are to be used.

I have an intense desire to go to the sick, and lay hands on them in the name of Jesus Christ and pray with them. I don't know if this is the beginning of another gift or if because of seventeen years of sickness and suffering I want so badly to help the sick. But, I'm not concerned for God knows and in His time, I will know.

This, I am sure of: He tells us that if you ask for anything in complete faith, it's yours. Last week our little Buffy got something in the yard that poisoned her. When I let her in, I realized that she was violently ill. She was frothing and vomiting with every step she took. I asked the Lord to save her. I loved her so much. As the hours went by, she was, in my opinion, near death. She could barely walk. I couldn't believe that, tiny as she was, her body could continue losing fluid, for she had wretched and vomited for hours. I said, "Lord, I'm not taking her to the vet, I know you can save her. If I took her to the vet, I'd be admitting to you and myself, and to the devil that I didn't have faith in You to heal her."

After many hours I knew something had to be done. She would soon be dehydrated and was now unable to walk. I got down beside her on the living room floor and I approached the throne of God boldly as He tells us to do. I placed my hands on Buffy, and said,

"Father, I'm coming boldly to your throne, carrying my little dog. You promised us that if we came to you with a pure heart, you would receive us and give us the desires of our hearts. Father, if my heart is not pure, I ask forgiveness and ask you to purify it, and I know that you will heal Buffy. Thank you, in Jesus' name."

I lay Buffy down; nothing happened. I said, "Lord Jesus, please show me that you heard me and healed her." As I said this, Buffy got up and walked down the hall. I started to praise the Lord. She was walking. Then, she came running in the room carrying her favorite toy and wanting to play. I praised the Lord and played with her for hours. She not only was healed, but was even peppier than before she had gotten sick. When Bud stepped in the door, he said, "Quick tell me what happened today."

I said, "How did you know?"

He laughed and said, "Your face has a light."

Jesus was showing me that every time I come before Him with Buffy, I have the complete faith required to ask and expect a healing. But, with people, the human embarrassment has kept me from the complete "without a doubt" type of faith needed to come before God boldly, expecting, and receiving a healing. So, in the time ahead, God will show me His will, which is all I ever want: that God's will be my own will.

I am asking now for the gift of wisdom, for without wisdom, the other gifts are pure delight to me, but will not help build Christ's church. For we must have the wisdom to know how and when to use these gifts. We also must remember that these gifts, if flaunted before others, can hinder the church's growth, not build it.

We need wisdom to keep ourselves from using these gifts to suit our wills, instead of waiting until God's purpose unfolds before us. Therefore, I would admonish all who seek and receive gifts to pray for wisdom. God's promise is clear to me in James 1:5 (*Living*

Bible): "If you want to know what God wants you to do, ask Him and He will gladly tell you, for he is always ready to give a bountiful supply of wisdom to all who ask Him: He will not resent it." But, James 1:6 (*Living Bible*) also says, "But when you ask him, be sure that you really expect him to tell you. For a doubtful mind will be as unsettled as a wave of the sea that is driven and tossed by the wind."

Chapter Sixteen

LEE

This is a very special chapter, and for many months I could not write about it. But, today, our Lord gave it to me. I not only can write it down, but I have to tell of dear Lee and the Lord.

As a child and throughout all of my growing up years, I was blessed to be born into a big and loving family. My mother's sisters and brothers were not aunts and uncles to me but more like second parents. So the word cousin to me was and is just a word; we are all brothers and sisters. Perhaps closer than natural brothers and sisters.

One of my aunts was particularly close. I was just a little younger than her four boys. This is about her third-born son, Lee.

As a child, Lee was not as close to me as were the other three boys. But, in later years, he became closer. Last September Lee was in a car accident. There were no injuries on his body, but a hard crack on the head had caused brain damage. He lay in his bed unconscious. Would he live? Only God knew that. Week after week went by—no response. He opened his eyes, but they were blank, unseeing it seemed. Hundreds of people from all the local churches were praying for him. Still he lay there.

At Thanksgiving, my mother, sister, Bud and I drove to see him. I must tell this the way I felt at the time, but bear in mind as you read this, that I would learn and grow in Christ in the months to come, so my thoughts at that particular time were not necessarily my thoughts as they stand now. Each day with Christ is new and exciting, because we know more than the day before. He opens our hearts, and shows us more and more.

As I followed my sister into Lee's room, my heart just broke, and I cried out, "Oh sweet Jesus!" During the months that he lay there, his weight had fallen and the man I saw was only skin and bones. He tossed and tried to move, but one side of his body was paralyzed and would not move. What tore my heart out was the fear that he seemed to feel. He was like a poor little animal that cruel people had trapped. Oh sweet Jesus, help him.

His eyes were open and staring, but blank and unknowing. He didn't know us. He was afraid. He tried to move away. He was trapped. My sister Donna sat beside the head of the bed, and I stayed at the bottom. Mom and Bud were at the sides, and Donna in her soft voice started to speak.

"Lee, Jesus loves you." On and on her voice went, but it wasn't really her voice. It was Jesus speaking through her. We all were praying. I can't speak for the feelings of the others, but I will never forget how I felt. Jesus seemed to tell me, "Lay you hand on him and tell him that it's OK. Don't be afraid." Donna's voice carried on, but I didn't hear her words any longer. I placed my hand on Lee's leg and in a soft voice (I have a grating, loud voice) said, "Lee, it's going to be OK. It's alright. Lee."

His tossing tortured body became still and the blank eyes seemed to fasten on my face. I closed my eyes and begged, "Oh, please Jesus, open his mind. If only one word can penetrate, let it be your sweet name. Let the name of Jesus enter that tormented mind." It was done.

How do I know? How dare I make a statement like that? Because my Lord said, "It is done." I knew that the name of Jesus was with Lee. I became aware of the room again, and Lee was still staring in my face. Jesus, Donna, Lee and I were alone in that room. I turned and looked into the hall. Bud was there crying, arms raised, telling Lee's mother that Jesus was in that room. "He's in there, I felt Him, Lee's going to be OK."

Soon we all gathered around the bed to lay our hands on him and ask Jesus for his healing. I had my hands on his head, and as we all started to pray, I realized that I was pressing quite hard on that dear head. How long did we pray? I don't know. When you're talking to Jesus, time means nothing. I lifted my hand as we said Amen. I wish that I could say for Lee's sake and for his family that he was healed. That he got up and walked out of that room. That was not the case. But he *was* still. It seemed as if some of the panic in his eyes was gone. We left the hospital.

Donna said, "He is healed."

I said only, "I know that the name of Jesus is in his heart."

When we returned home, we asked people to pray for Lee. We all prayed every day. My prayers were, "Oh, dear Jesus, I place Lee before you and I beg for his healing. Only you can heal him. There is no one on earth that can help him. Please Jesus. Thank you."

You see we always end our prayers with "Thank you." We believe Jesus will answer, so we thank Him ahead of time. Why wait. We might forget.

We kept in close contact with Lee's mother. Praise the Lord. Lee was responding. His sister and brother flew in from Texas and his eyes followed them as they moved about the room and they felt that he knew them. The doctor decided to move him to a hospital in another part of the State. That was unfortunate. When his family went to see him, they found him dirty, bruised and in pain. By then the Lord had opened Lee's mouth. He could utter a few simple words. He asked to go home. It was impossible. They had him moved back to a hospital closer to home. Somehow, his hip had been broken and he was again in pain.

By now it was March. Donna, Mom and I went to Pennsylvania and of course we went to see Lee. Oh, how my heart leaped with joy when I saw him. The last time that I had seen him there was no hope for him, except through Jesus. Oh, he was even thinner, one side paralyzed, and his neck still paralyzed, but his eyes! They were no longer blank. He knew me!

His mother said, "Lee, do you know who this is?"

After a few moments, looking right at me, he said, "Yes, it's Alice."

"How are you?" he asked.

"Just fine," I answered.

In a few minutes he spoke again. "Not sick?"

Realizing that he was referring to me, I answered, "No, I've been healed."

You see, before his accident, I was just being healed after seventeen years and he did not know anything about this nor could he have known of my salvation. I laid my hand on his head and said, "God bless you, Lee." His head tried to raise, and I moved my hand thinking he was uncomfortable. What he actually wanted, was to feel my touch. His eyes kept darting from my cross on my chest to my own eyes and back again. Let me take the time to explain just why I wear a cross. First of all, it proclaims to the world that Jesus Christ is my Lord, and second, my sins died on that cross. I am reborn. It is a constant reminder.

Back to Lee. He kept looking at my cross, then to my eyes. I felt that he was trying so hard to tell me with his eyes what he could not speak. But what? There was no way that he cound remember last November. Was there? He tires very quickly, so I said, "Lee would you like to sleep?"

He answered, "Yes." Then he shouted a word. I thought it was—pray. But Lee would never ask me to pray. Would he? He didn't know that I had been reborn, he only knew the old Alice. I asked him again what he said, and his answer was, "Pray."

"Do you want us to pray for you?" I asked.

"Yes," he answered quietly.

Again, we gathered around his bed as we approached our Lord on behalf of Lee. Again peace entered those dear eyes. Can you leave someone you love, in that condition, and be wondrously happy? Yes. My heart swelled with joy. Lee knew Jesus. He would be healed.

On the ride home, I relived those minutes, happy in knowing that Jesus was with Lee and realizing that when I had laid my hand on his head, asking God's blessing, Lee hadn't been uncomfortable as I had thought. He was trying to again feel that pressure during prayer he had felt in November.

In May Bud and I went again to Pennsylvania to see him. This time his brother, sister and mother went along with us. We found him sitting in a chair. True, he was tied there, and was still paralyzed, but the joy again hit my heart. His eyes looked at Bud and I and he not only knew us, his dear face sent us the message. When Jesus dwells inside any of us, we have a communication with others of the Lord that need no spoken word. Before we left, I knelt before him. Since I had seen him last, he had been flown to Denver, Colorado for testing. The results showed that he would never be anything or any better than he was now. Nothing could be done for him. So he had been brought to this rest home. Lee knew what had been said, and seemed to have given up all hope. So, as I knelt there, I told him from my heart, "Lee, I pray for you every day. I will never stop, nor will I ever give up. I will keep on praying for you and you pray too, OK?"

I did not expect any answer, and to my joy, he looked in my eyes and said, "I will."

Oh, Lord, he is yours. Thank you Lord. All he needs is a little time to really learn about you. Thank you Lord!

Now that his mind was open, I could write him short simple notes, opening up the world of Jesus to him. In June, my mother and Donna went to see Lee. I sent a small framed picture of Jesus to him. When they arrived, he seemed to be losing the use of his other arm. He had been to therapy and was exhausted. He could not, or would not, talk: not even the few words that he had been capable of speaking. Obviously he was just too tired to stay awake, so mother and Donna, along with his sisters and brothers who had also come to visit decided to leave and let him get some rest.

Before she left, Donna knelt before Lee, showing the picture to him, telling him that I had sent it and she explained who it was and just what Jesus was and that Jesus loved him and was with him. She then placed the picture on the stand facing Lee where he could look at it, when slowly, so painfully, Lee's hand started to move toward that nightstand and, as all watched, with seemingly superhuman effort, his hand kept moving until, at last it could reach the picture of Jesus. He held it in his hand. What was in his mind?

I began the chapter telling you that I couldn't write about Lee. Why? Well, I felt that he would be healed and I wanted to wait till I could tell of his victory over illness. Why can I write now? Now I know how very big Lee's victory really is. Yes, he's still bound in that poor tormented body, but he has gained the biggest victory that anyone can have. He has God's promise of a new life—a life in which he will have a new body, a body that, will never again, through all eternity feel anything but great joy.

My prayers are now, "Thank you for the healing of Lee's soul. I place him before You. He is one of yours, oh Lord, give him peace and healing of his physical body. Help his family in their love and worry for Lee. Show us all Your will and praise your Holy name."

I still pray that Lee will be healed. But I know that Lee is in God's hands. Is there any better place to be? "Now we are Christ's. We are the true descendants of Abraham, and *all* God's promises to him belong to us." Galatians 3:29, *Living Bible*.

Added reassurance comes from I Peter 5:10 (*Living Bible*). "After you have suffered a little while, our God, who is full of kindness through Christ will give you His eternal glory, He personally will come and pick you up and sit you firmly in place, and make you stronger than ever."

Also remember "you can get anything, anything you ask for in prayer—*if you believe*." Matthew 2:22, *Living Bible*.

God's promises follow Lee from this world into the next. What a comfort it is to read these words, "First we have these human bodies. Later God gives us spiritual, heavenly bodies." I Corinthians 15:46, *Living Bible*. "When he comes back, he will take these dying bodies of ours and change them into glorious bodies like His own, using the great power he will use to conquer all else everywhere." Philippians 3:21, *Living Bible*.

Thank you, Jesus!!!

Chapter Seventeen

COME AS A CHILD

My faith in the Lord can be compared to the trust and faith that a little child has for his parents. I believe that Jesus has the answer for everything. I believe that Jesus hears all of my thoughts and prayers. I believe that Jesus knows what I need even before I do, and supplies those needs. I believe that Jesus answers all prayers. I believe that Jesus gives us more than our own heart's desire. I also believe that we must come to Him as a child. In Mark 10:15, Jesus says, "I tell you as seriously as I know how that anyone who refuses to come to God as a child can not enter the kingdom of Heaven."

Come as a child to Jesus. Do not be afraid to give up what you guard as your independence. Do you really want to make all your decisions? Big and small. Do you want the burden of making a wrong decision? Think about this. As a child, so long ago, wasn't it nice, not to have to worry and make decisions? Isn't it a great relief to let Jesus decide instead of you? He never makes mistakes, as we do.

Think back to your childhood. Did you have an unseen playmate as most children have? I did. No one else could see that perfect playmate but me. We talked, laughed and played all day. I could tell my imaginary friend anything. He never got angry at me, never left my side, and always loved me. Doesn't this friend sound like Jesus Christ? Do you have something on your mind that you just can't tell anyone about? Try telling Jesus. He knows already. He will listen.

Remember those childhood diseases? Measles, colds, chicken pox, etc.? What was the best part of being sick? Wasn't it the special love and attention from your parents? When you hurt they hurt. When you were sick, they worried and fussed over you. Now, when you are truly sick and in pain, do your loved ones really know how you feel? They can't, it's impossible. But, Jesus knows exactly how you feel. His love will heal you.

When you were a child, did you ever think or worry about a job, money or sickness? Did any of these adult anathemas ever plague you? No. Children, for the most part, simply love and trust their parents, and I myself was no different. Do you feel that now, as an adult, that you have to worry about these things? If you do worry about them, can you change anything at all by worrying. Read what Luke has to say about worrying, in Chapter 12 verses 25-27. Verse 25 says it in a nutshell: "What's the use of worrying? What good does it do? Will it add a single day to your life?" (*Living Bible*.)

To use a perfect example of a child's faith, I would like to share this true experience related to me by a Christian brother, Gene. His five-year-old niece was playing upstairs and her mother was taking a rest on the porch when her daughter called, "Mommy, we have a visitor." Now mommy listened with a smile, because she was on the porch, and would certainly have noticed any visitors, so she called to the little girl, "Who is our visitor?" The answer was one word, "Jesus!" Needless to say, that must have shaken the mother a bit, but staying cool, she answered, "I'll be right in." And do you know what the little girl answered, "No, that's OK, He only came to talk to me."

That is what I mean by the faith of a child: Complete innocence and trust. Oh, if only we could all have her love of Jesus. Do you really believe that Jesus was upstairs with her? I do.

Wouldn't life be so much sweeter as a child again? Wouldn't you like to know that every decision facing you is already being taken care of, by the best authority in the world? Do you hesitate to talk to Jesus about what you think may be just a little thing? It's not a little thing to the Lord; if it has upset you, then it's a big thing to Him and you should talk to Him about it. He's right there. Turn to Jesus today, before it is too late. Let the love of Christ heal you spiritually as well as physically. Go as a child. Find a new life waiting just for you. Jesus is waiting for you right now.

Chapter Eighteen

THE BEGINNING OF THE LORD'S BOOK

Shortly after Buffy's healing, the Lord seemed to be saying to me, "Write a book." Each time that I answered, "Lord you made me—you know me better than even I know myself. You know that I can't do this." But more and more, every day, then several times a day, I got the message, "Write a book."

"Lord please," I said. I had never said "no" to Him, but I was always bad in spelling, with not too much formal education. Me? Write a book? "No Lord, not me." Stronger and stronger, it came, "Write it down." Remember how Moses said no over and over to God?

I prayed many times. "Lord how?" I asked. "Is it of You, these thoughts?" As I argued with the Lord about it, a friend dropped in, and we naturally discussed the glory of the Lord, and suddenly I found myself telling her of my burden for writing a book glorifying the Lord. Colleen's face glowed. Something clicked in her head. Excitedly she told me that just a few days earlier, Kate had confided to her that she felt the terrible urge to write for the glory of Jesus, but could not find a beginning, nor a basis on which to found a book. I said, "Tell her of my burden and we will all pray about it."

We did. I called Kate and we agreed that I would pray for the writing and she, having a great deal of time, would correct and type it all. You can see that God has been in control at all times. He told me to write it. He laid a burden on Kate to type it, and he arranged a Stanley party for us to get together. Months later, Kate mentioned to me that she had a feeling about me the first night we had met. She said, "There was something in your voice and your look, when you mentioned your cross around your neck, that got me to thinking: is this lady a re-born Christian?"

So, as the good Lord had planned, we got together, and started the first in a series of long discussions about the wonderful things that Jesus had done for us, and our hopes for the future and our confidence in the Lord. As I unfolded my story about the book, I also mentioned to Kate that there was one part of my experience that I was unable to write about, or for that matter, even talk about with any confidence. Very quietly she said, "You can tell me about it, if you want to, and I will try to write it down." I proceeded to tell her of the vision of Jesus that I had when Cindy was just a baby. Now, I never told anyone about this for many many years, and only since I found Jesus, have I told Bud, but yet, here I was, telling this young girl, someone I barely knew about a vision of Jesus. I had tried to tell others of it, but even in telling Bud, I could not get a grip on the whole thing; but when Kate asked me to tell her, the words just flowed out of my mouth. Not once did I even stop to gather my thoughts, so clearly did the recollection of that night so long ago come back to me. This was a turning point for Kate. It was then she knew, that this book was of the Lord, and I wasn't kidding her. She knew then, just what to write. So, with a notebook full of my handwritten details of my long illnesses, we began to put together the pieces of this story, calling each other frequently and delighting together in the glory of our Lord.

The book progressed rapidly and it was typed in

three weeks. Eagerly I took it and gave it to Hank, Donna, Bud, Cindy and a few others to read, and give their opinions. Anxiously, we waited and when Kate called me the next week, she could immediately sense the disappointment in my voice.

"How did they like it?" she asked.

"Well, not too well," I replied. I was too despondent to even want to go into details with her.

Crushed, she went on, "Well, what was the matter with it? You and I know that it is of the Lord, and that He wants it done. Maybe, he just doesn't want me to work on it with you." She began blaming herself. Perhaps she thought that the writing style had turned them off. I hurried to explain.

"No," I assured her. "They all say that it's a wonderful testimony, but it just doesn't make a complete book. I don't know where to go from here." We were sure that this book was of God. Were we wrong? We would pray about it. We hit bottom. We had been so very sure that God had said to write. But God doesn't make mistakes, so if this book were not of Him, then we had assumed too much.

We spent hours and days and finally weeks praying still; all we could really feel from God was, "I told you to write." I searched myself. Did I really want to write this book. How could I? It showed the real me—a sinner. Did I expect to make money? Of course not. I believe that God takes care of all my needs. Did I enjoy having people, especially my family and friends laugh at me for trying to do the impossible? Hardly.

But, I felt that this book really told what a great and merciful Lord we serve. How abundant was His pity and love for me those seventeen years. I feel that Mark, Chapter 5, verse 26 best expresses the way I was. "She had suffered much from many doctors through the years and had become poor from paying them, and was no better but, in fact, was worse." How I must have tried

His patience as He waited for me to come to Him as He knew that I would. "But God had mercy on me so that Christ Jesus could use me as an example to show everyone how patient he is with even the worst sinners, so that others will realize that they, too, can have everlasting life." I Timothy 1:16.

For two months, I prayed and begged the Lord to show me His will for this book. Still no progress was made. You don't know how much I wanted to toss it all aside and forget about. But, I couldn't. I just could not forget about this book! Kate had been doing her own soul searching and praying and as we talked together we agreed.

We believe in God's will being done, as scripture tells us. We believe that with God, all things are possible. We can say thank you Lord, for these last weeks. Our faith was tested and you brought us through and strengthened our faith even more. How could we possibly think of failure, when God's will was guiding us? We had nothing to lose and so much to gain. Praise God that He kept us at it!

Maybe we should rewrite it and try again," I said.

"Alright," Kate said, "go ahead and rewrite it and I'll type it over and we'll start again. It shouldn't take too long." Poor Kate—little did she know just how long it would be.

Even though we were both discouraged, we didn't give up. I tried to convince Kate that the Lord certainly did want her to work on it with me, otherwise, He wouldn't have thrown us together so conveniently. As the weeks turned into months, I finished my part of the rewrite, and Kate started typing again. She did very well, until she came to the last three chapters, and then received a wonderful promotion, which occupied most of her former typing time, and the book lay in her desk untouched for many weeks. I called periodically to check on the progress, and each time she would answer, "You know, it's the strangest thing; I know that you think that the Lord wants me to work on this with you, but I really can't seem to find the time. It's almost as if He's trying to keep me from it." I just told her to keep trying, that the Lord did want her to do the work, and that I wanted her to do it, and I would wait and perhaps even bring a typewriter to her home so that she could type it after work.

"Alright," she said. "I'll stick with it."

The next week, I picked up the phone, and heard an excited Kate on the other end. "Guess what!" she said. "I've been able to type the last chapters of the book, and I'll drop it off to you tonight."

Imagine her surprise, when I said, "Guess what I've got to tell you. A couple of days ago, I got the urge to write again, and I began thinking, that the book tells of my healing, but in no way does it tell of the wonderful life I now have through Jesus. The good Lord was holding us up on purpose, so that I could learn these things, and experience these things, and pass them on to be typed and added to the book."

"Praise the Lord!" she screeched. "What a relief! You're right, absolutely right!" In just a few minutes those words turned us completely around, and with new confidence I began more writing, and she started to type once more. This time the typing went smoothly; no interruptions occurred.

We know now, that we will never again allow those around us to shut out the voice of God. We know that God has a place for this book and knowing that He will take charge of everything and show us where and why He wants it written is all that is necessary.

You, who are reading this, can see the power of Jesus, simply in the publication of this book.

Now, we feel that the book will be completed. We have learned to praise the Lord in all things, even the bad, because He *is* in control, and He always does what is best for us. We have gained many blessings as we talked with each other for hours and hours. We have found out just how very rich we are. "Do you want to be truly rich? You already are if you are happy and good. After all, we didn't bring any money with us when we came into the world, and we can't carry away a single penny when we die" I Timothy 6:6-7 (*Living Bible*).

Our joint desire for this book is summed up for us in I Timothy 6:13-14: "I command you before God who gives life to all and before Christ Jesus who gave a fearless testimony before Pontius Pilate that you fulfill all He has told you to do, so that no one can find fault with you from now on, until our Lord Jesus Christ returns."

Our part of it is done, and now I feel that His book will be started. Started? Yes, started. Any book about the Lord can never be finished; His work is unending. Praise the Lord! Thank you, Jesus.